AF305187

ITALO MUSSA

STEPHANIE OURSLER

5 CUTS

Primo Tempo
(Untitled)
... losing all let her forget
He was romantic
... up in the air

Autobiografica, la Narrative Art di
Stephanie Oursler si svolge mediante
riferimenti indiretti, lontani sia
nel tempo che nello spazio. L'immagine
e il testo ne fanno una « esperienza
vissuta » (quella dell'artista)
proiettata e controllata dai tempi
della memoria volontaria.
Come in Le Gac, la narrazione si
prefigura spaziata, cioè su due
piani paralleli ma tra loro
divergenti. Anche perchè l'immagine
come il testo nel rifarsi al
« veduto » e al « vissuto » agiscono,
su di noi, prospetticamente. Infatti
mentre il testo indaga sul passato,
l'immagine ha una sua attualità,
sottratta in tempi diversi,
re-inventata dalla memoria volontaria.
Seguiamo da vicino le sequenze
narrative dei « 5 Cuts ».
Primo Tempo comprende l'infanzia,
recuperata attraverso fatti personali
ed eventi storici. Un esempio: **Sua
madre è morta che lei aveva due anni.
Poco dopo, lo stesso anno, l'America
entrò in guerra.**

Le immagini sono: palcoscenico, cantante,
orchestra; treno affollato, confusione
tra la folla che parte e saluta.
Sua madre... significa l'infanzia,
Poco dopo... prefigura l'avvenire.
Tra le due immagini c'è, però, una
differenza visiva: nitida la prima,
graffiata la seconda. Poi lo
svolgimento della narrazione procede
marcando, via via, il divaricamento
o l'abbinamento tra il fatto personale
e l'evento storico.
Senza titolo. È un filmato di
tutto ciò che, per la protagonista,
significa apprendimento impersonale.
Qui il testo sorregge l'immagine,
perchè non deve nè prefigurare
l'avvenire nè registrare l'infanzia.
Tra immagine e testo si stabilisce
un rapporto riduttivo, astratto e
tanto indiretto da distoglierci
da ogni manifestazione di
divaricamento o abbinamento tra
il fatto personale e l'evento
storico. Non a caso, a questo punto,
la narrazione è senza titolo.
Perdeva tutto e dimenticava tutto.

L'infanzia è scomparsa, la
prefigurazione dell'avvenire
prende, d'ora in poi, il sopravvento.
Un esempio: **Non le piacevano mai le
sue case, perdeva tutto e dimenticava
tutto. Grumi di sangue erano saliti
al polmone. Altri le avevano eliminato
le due gambe.** Le immagini sono: interno
con figure; figure sedute sull'erba.
Qui l'analogia tra il testo e la
immagine presenta una lettura
indecifrabile, surrealisticamente
enigmatica. Questo « non-sense » linguistico
è solo apparente, poichè la parola
« tutto » compie una specie di
azzeramento alla memoria volontaria,
evitandogli, però, significati
fuorvianti.
Lui era romantico. Il fatto è preciso,
da collegare alla « esperienza vissuta »
in tutta la sua complessa
articolazione esistenziale: l'amore,
la passione politica, il rifiuto
di ogni manifestazione trionfalistica
della vita.
Il fatto è, dunque, preciso perchè
indica un carattere formatosi dal

« basso », vicino a tutto ciò che
agli altri sembrava troppo semplice,
troppo insignificante.
Per aria, infine, rappresenta la sintesi
del personale e della storia, vista,
per analogia, attraverso l'ottica del
veduto-vissuto.
Un esempio: **Incontrò un meccanico
greco mentre stava cercando una Porsche
Li lasciò tutti per aria.**
Le immagini sono: una coppia (di amanti?)
che si bacia intensamente; e un dirigibile
per aria. Tutto ciò che è, sfugge e si
dissolve nello spazio della vita; ma solo
così si ottiene la piena libertà,
che trasforma il tempo (della memoria)
in sentire-ricordare, desiderare-soffrire,
esistere-morire.
Così la narrazione di Stephanie Oursler,
non avendo altri riferimenti che nei suoi
apparenti « non-senses » linguistici,
assume un significato sociologico in virtù
del valore attribuito a tutto
ciò che è altro da sé.

Italo Mussa

Autobiographical, the Narrative Art of
Stephanie Oursler unfolds itself by way of
indirect references, far away from both
time and space. The images
and the text themselves make a « lived
experience » (that of the artist)
projected and controlled by the times
of a voluntary memory.
As in Le Gac, the narration
prefigures itself spatially, that is on two
parallel levels but, between themselves,
diverging. Also, because both the image
and the text, by remaking the
« seen » and the « lived », act
upon us in the form of a perspective. In fact,
while the text investigates the past,
the image has its own actuality,
subtracted at different times,
re-invented from a voluntary memory.
Let us follow closely the narrative
sequences of « 5 CUTS ».
Primo Tempo includes infancy,
recovered through personal facts
and historical events. An example: **Her
mother died when she was 2. America entered
the war later that same year.**
The images are: stage, singer, orchestra;

crowded train, confusion among the crowd
that is departing and saluting.
Her mother... signifies infancy,
later... prefigures the future.
Between the two images, however, there's a
visual difference: neat the first,
scratched the second. Then, the
unfolding of the narration proceeds
marking, time by time, the spreading apart
or the combining among personal fact
and historical event.
(Untitled) is a film of
everything that, for the feminine protagonist,
signifies impersonal learning.
Here, the text supports the image
because it doesn't have to either prefigure
the future or record childhood.
Between image and text, there's established
a reduced rapport, abstract and
very indirect, turning away
every manifestation of
a spreading apart or a combining with
personal fact and historical event.
Not accidently, at this point,
the narration is untitled.
Losing all let her forget.
Childhood has disappeared, the

prefiguration of the future
takes, from now on, the helm.
An example: **She never liked her
homes; losing all let her forget.
Blood clots reached her lung. Others
had removed both legs.** The images are: interior
with figures; figures sitting on the grass.
Here, the analogy between the text and the
image presents an indecipherable
reading, surrealistically
enigmatic. This « non-sense » linguistic
is only seeming, since the word
« all » commits a sort of
zeroing in to the voluntary memory,
avoiding, however, misleading references.
He was romantic. The fact is precise,
connected to the « lived experience »
in all its complex
existential articulation: love,
political passion, the refusal
of every triumphalistic manifestation
of life.
The fact is, therefore, precise because
it indicates a character formed from
« below », close to all that
to others seems too simple,
too insignificant.

Up in the air, finally, represents the synthesis
of the personal and history, viewed,
by analogy, through the optics of
seen-lived.
An example: **She met a Greek mechanic
while looking for a Porsche.
She left them up in the air.**
The images are: a couple (lovers?)
kissing each other intensely; and a dirigible
up in the air. All that is, escapes and
dissolves in the space of life; but only
like this one gains the full liberty,
that transforms the time (of memory)
into to feel-to remember, to desire-to suffer,
to exist-to die.
In this way, the narration of Stephanie Oursler,
not having other references than in her
seemingly « non-sense » linguistics,
assumes a sociological significance by virtue
of the value attributed to all
that is other than apparent.

Italo Mussa

Primo Tempo

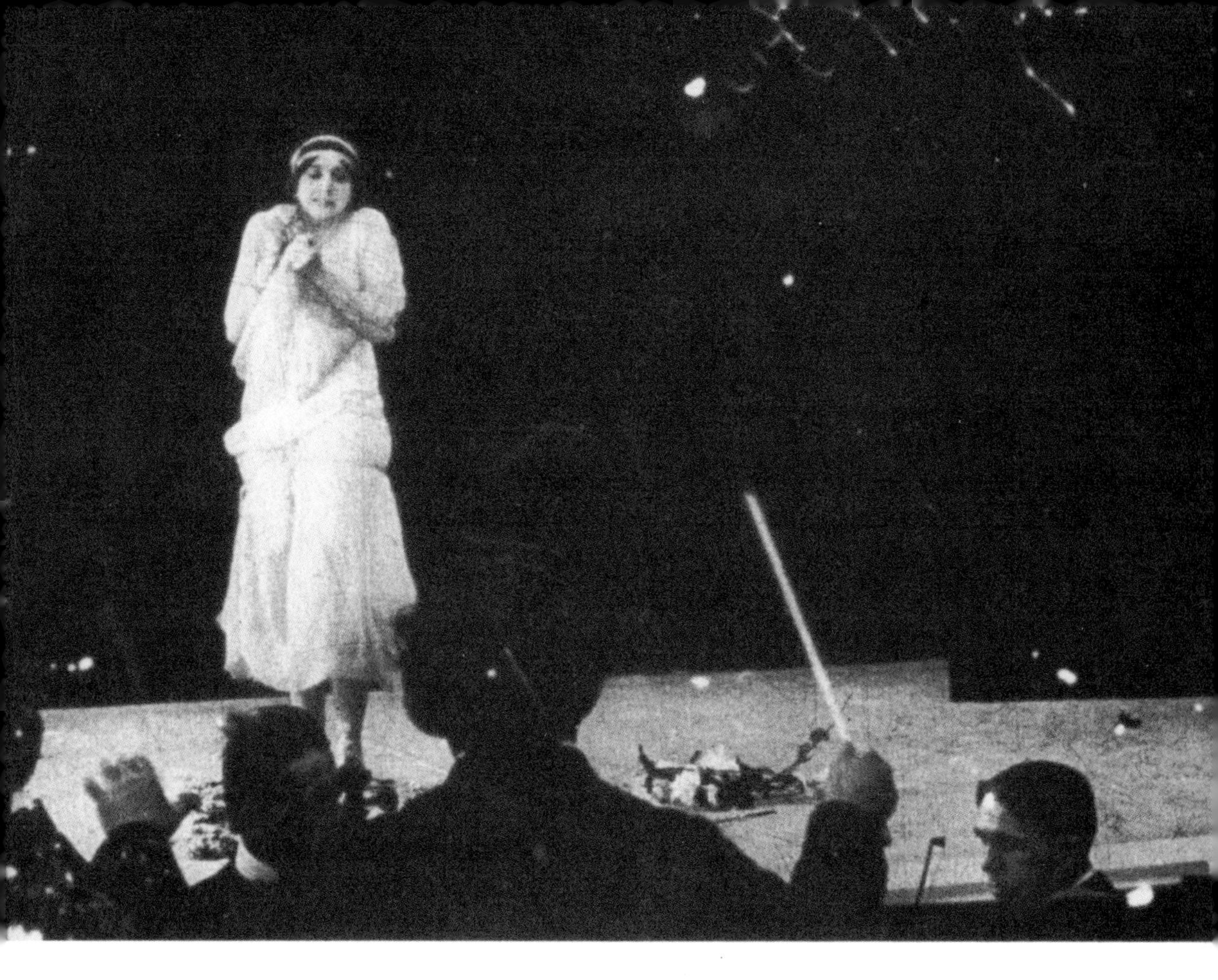

Her mother died
when she was 2

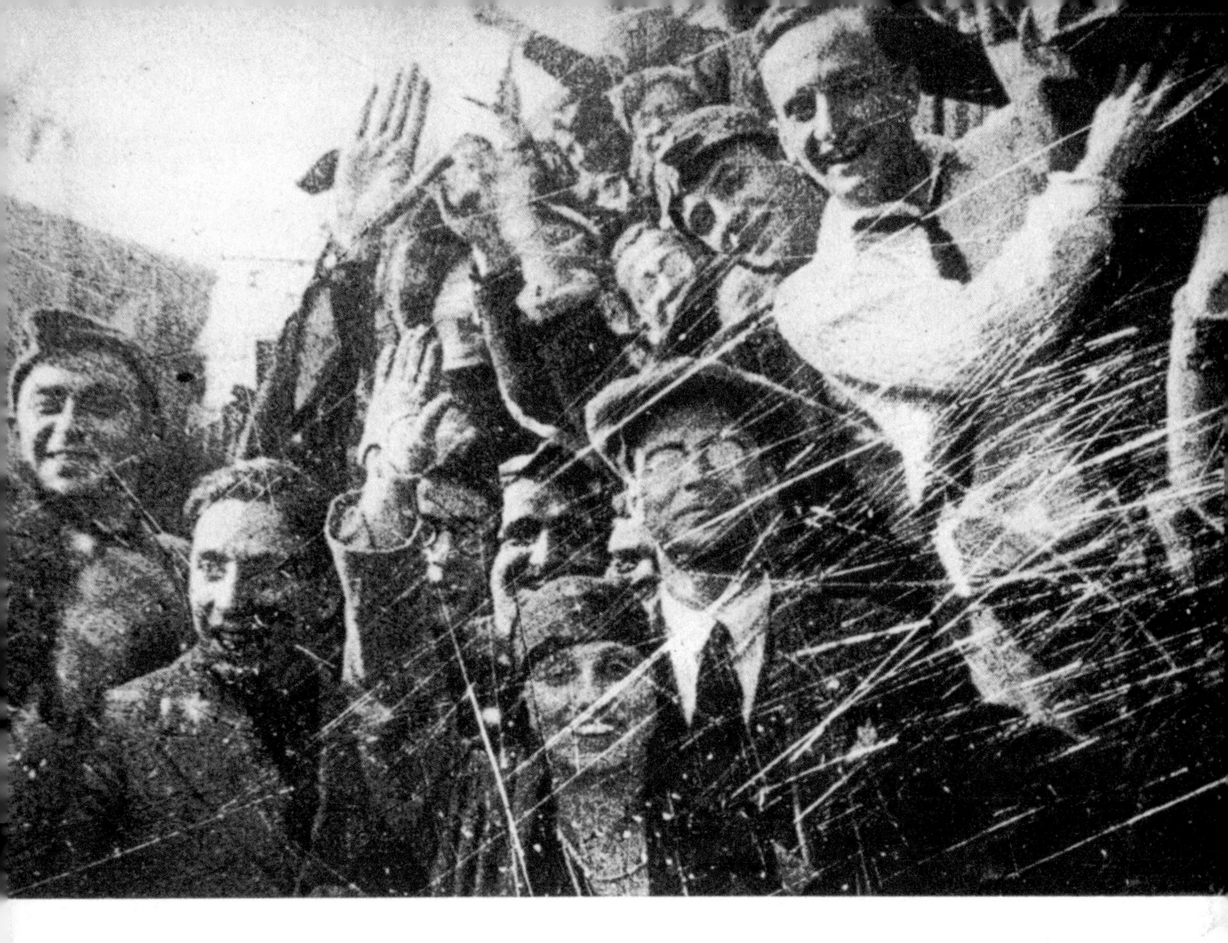

America entered the war
later that same year

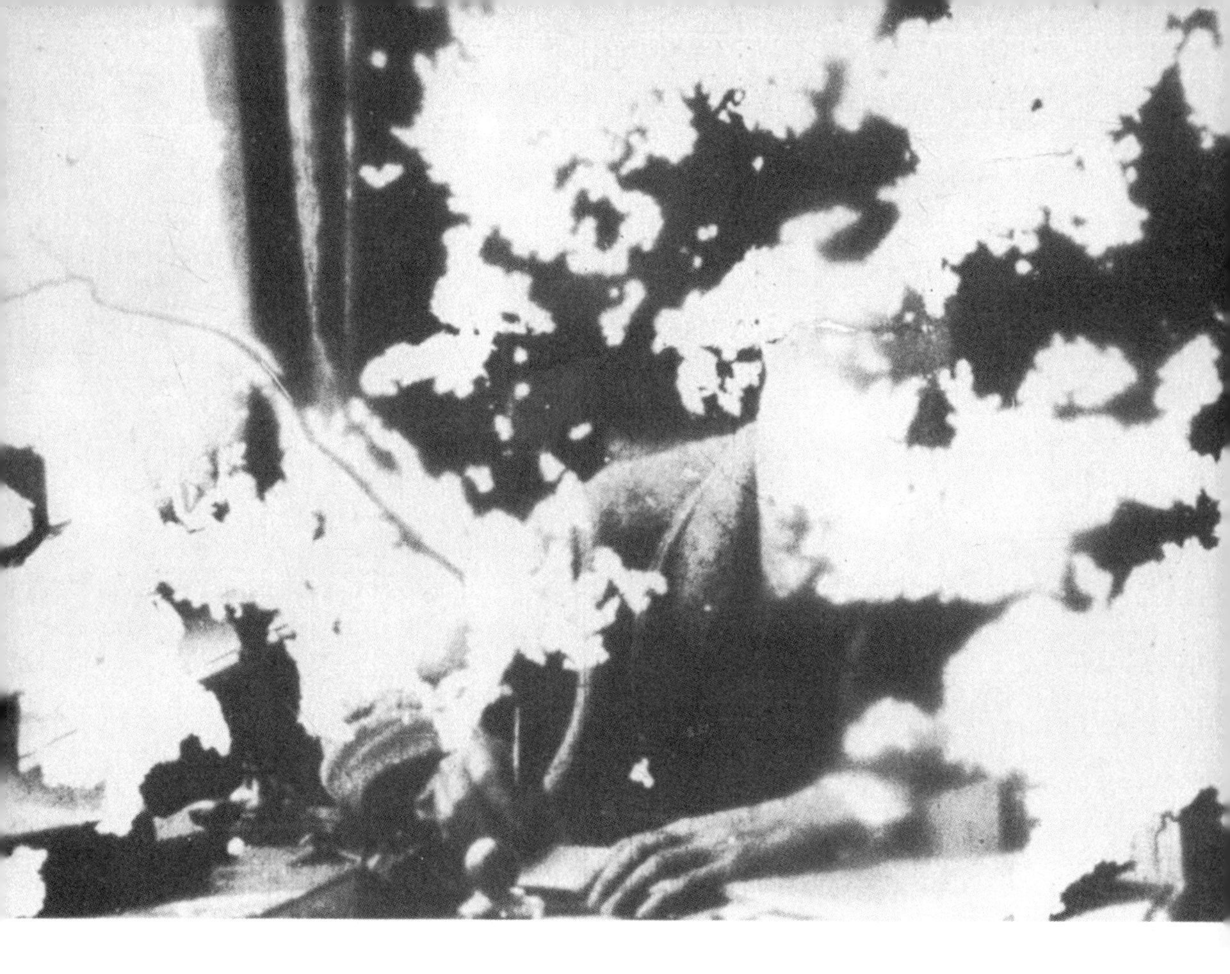

Her father died
when she was 9

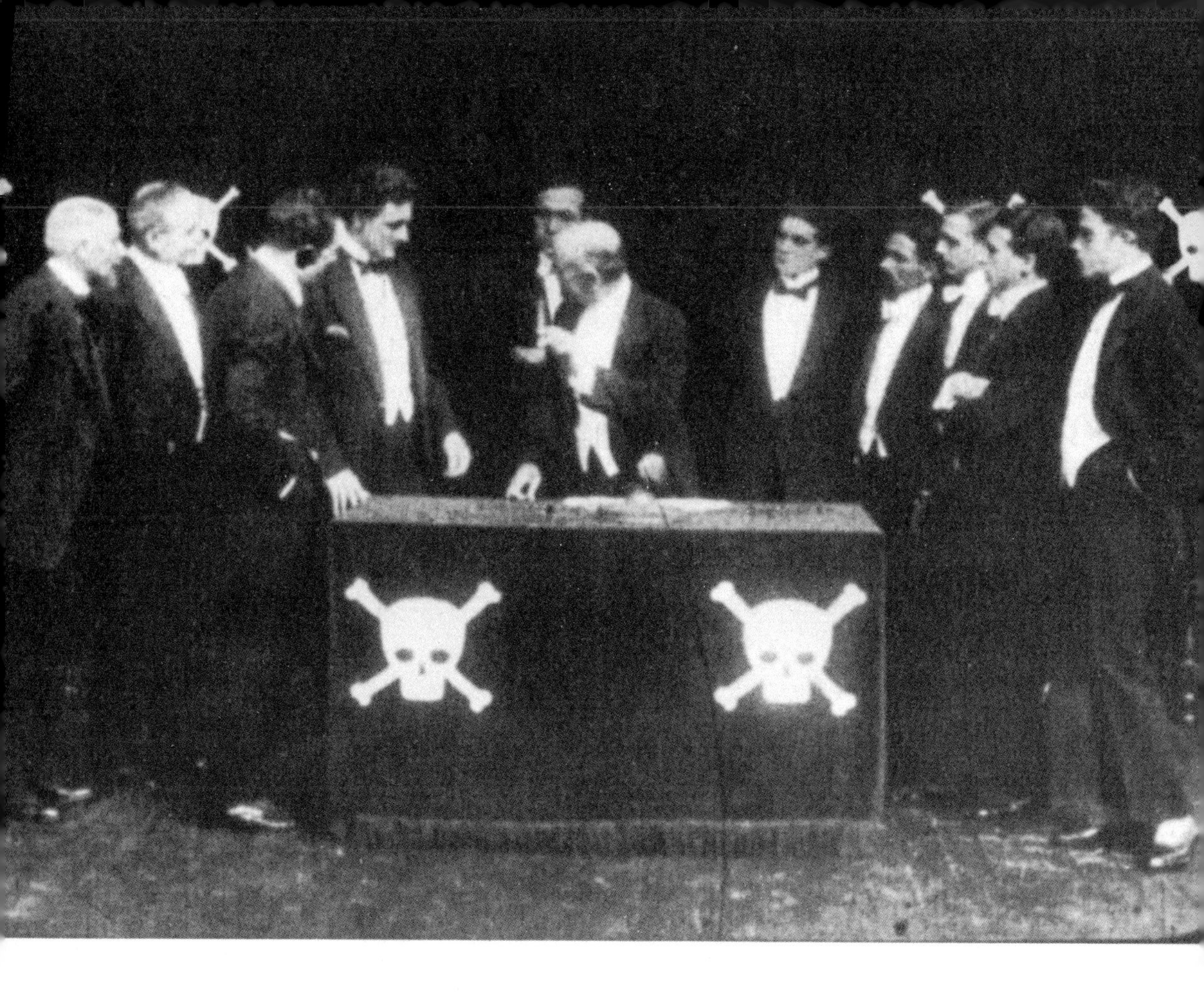

They were very sociable and
loved. She doesn't remember,

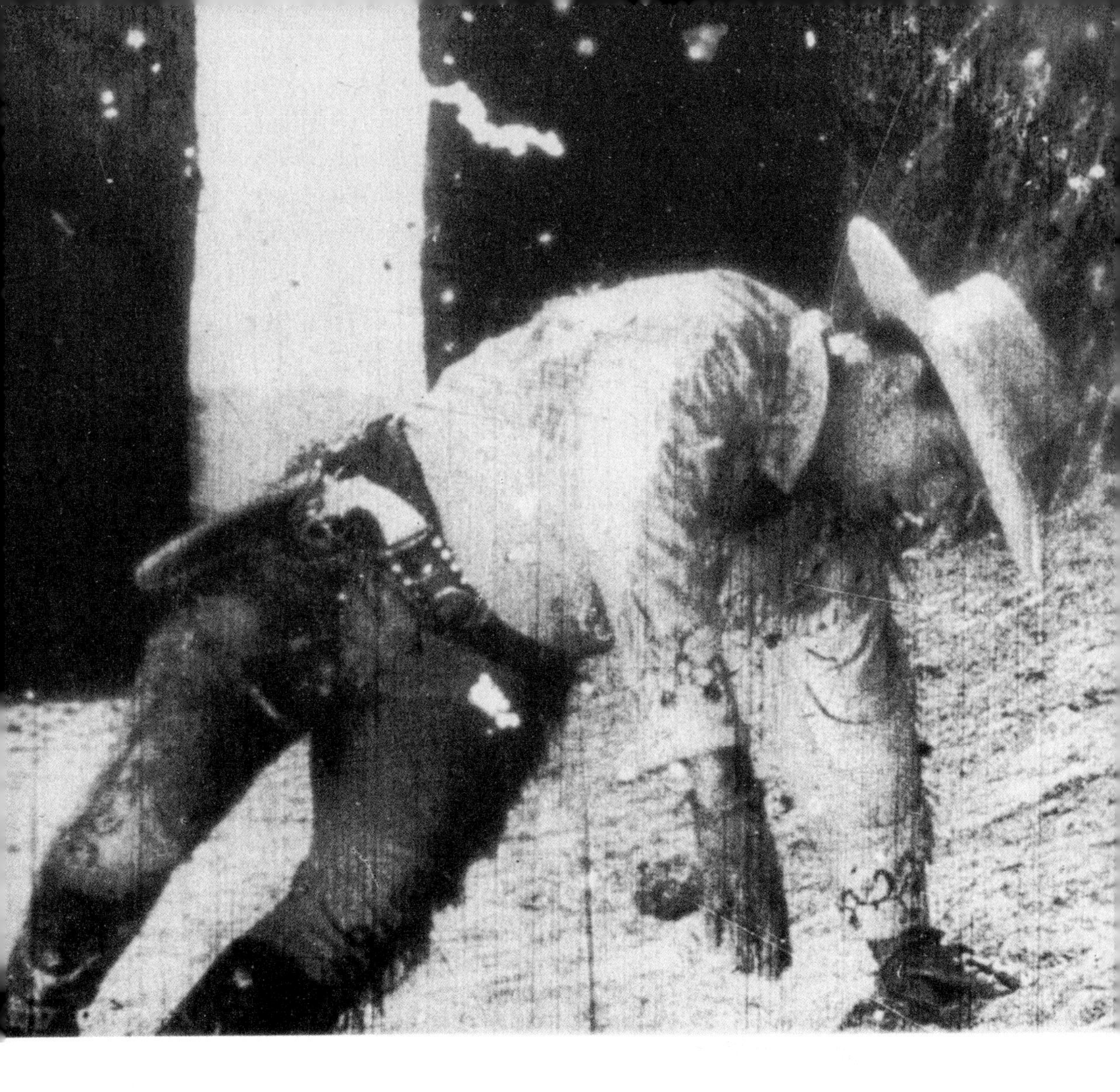

Later she continued to play
cowboys and indians.

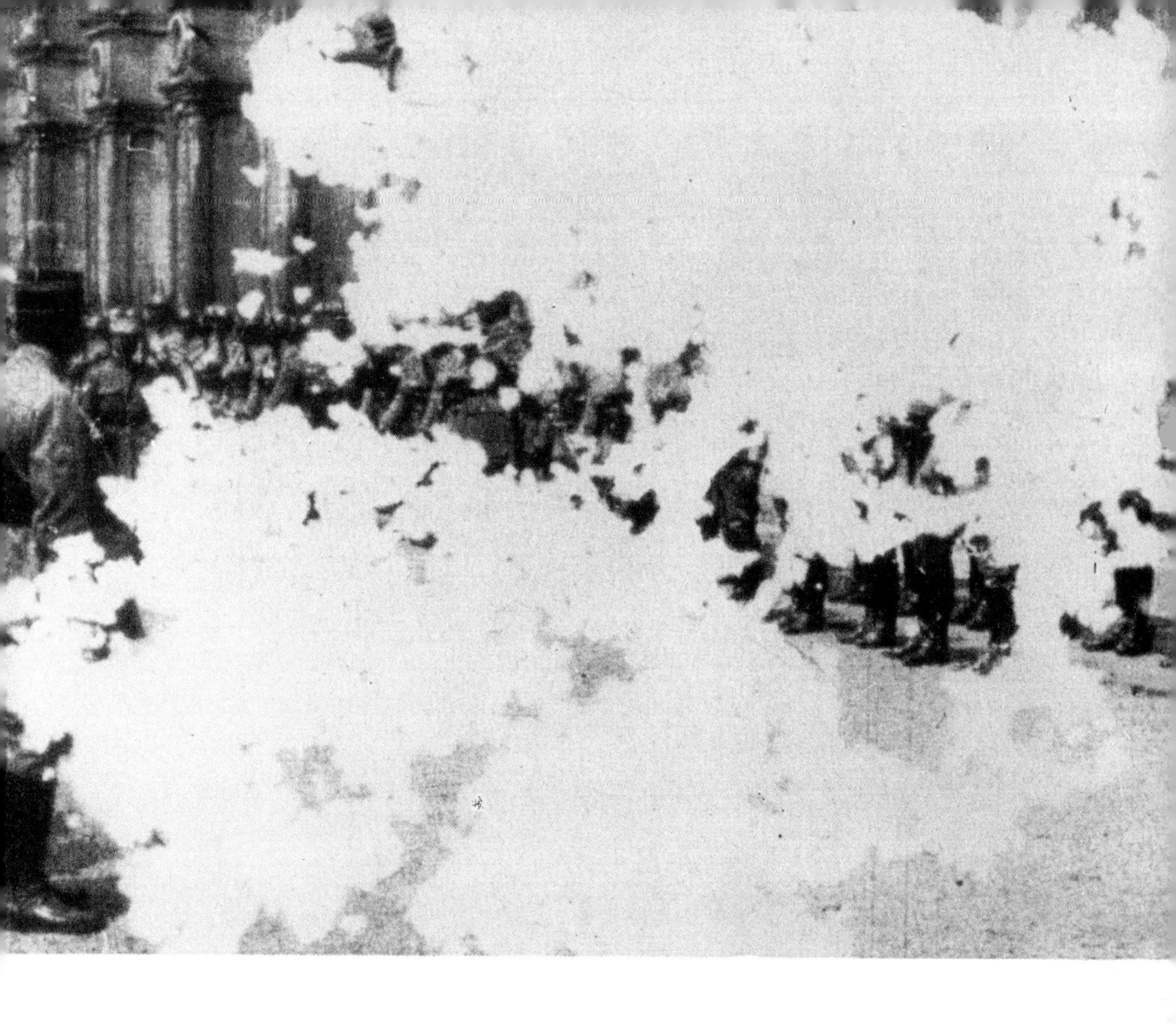

Parades passed,

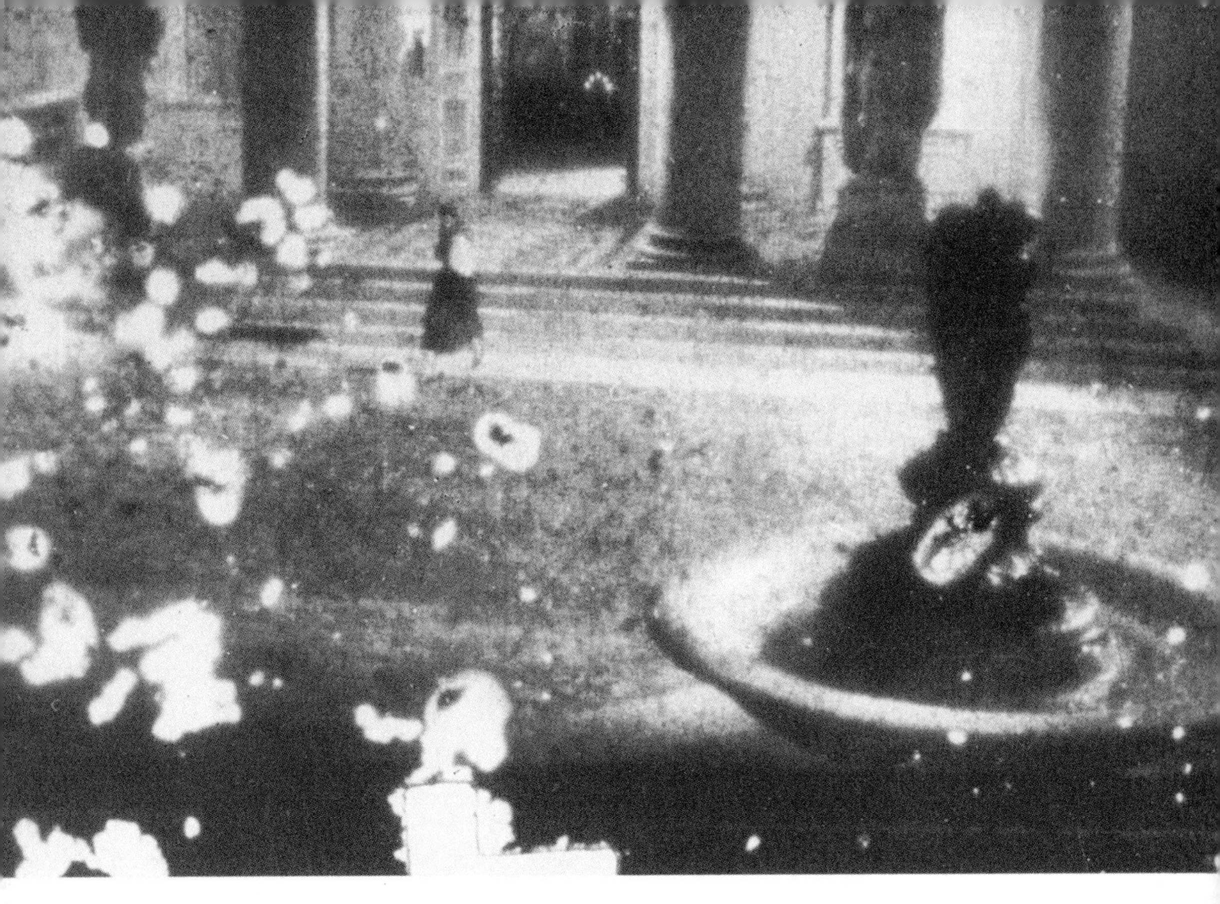

and many nights.

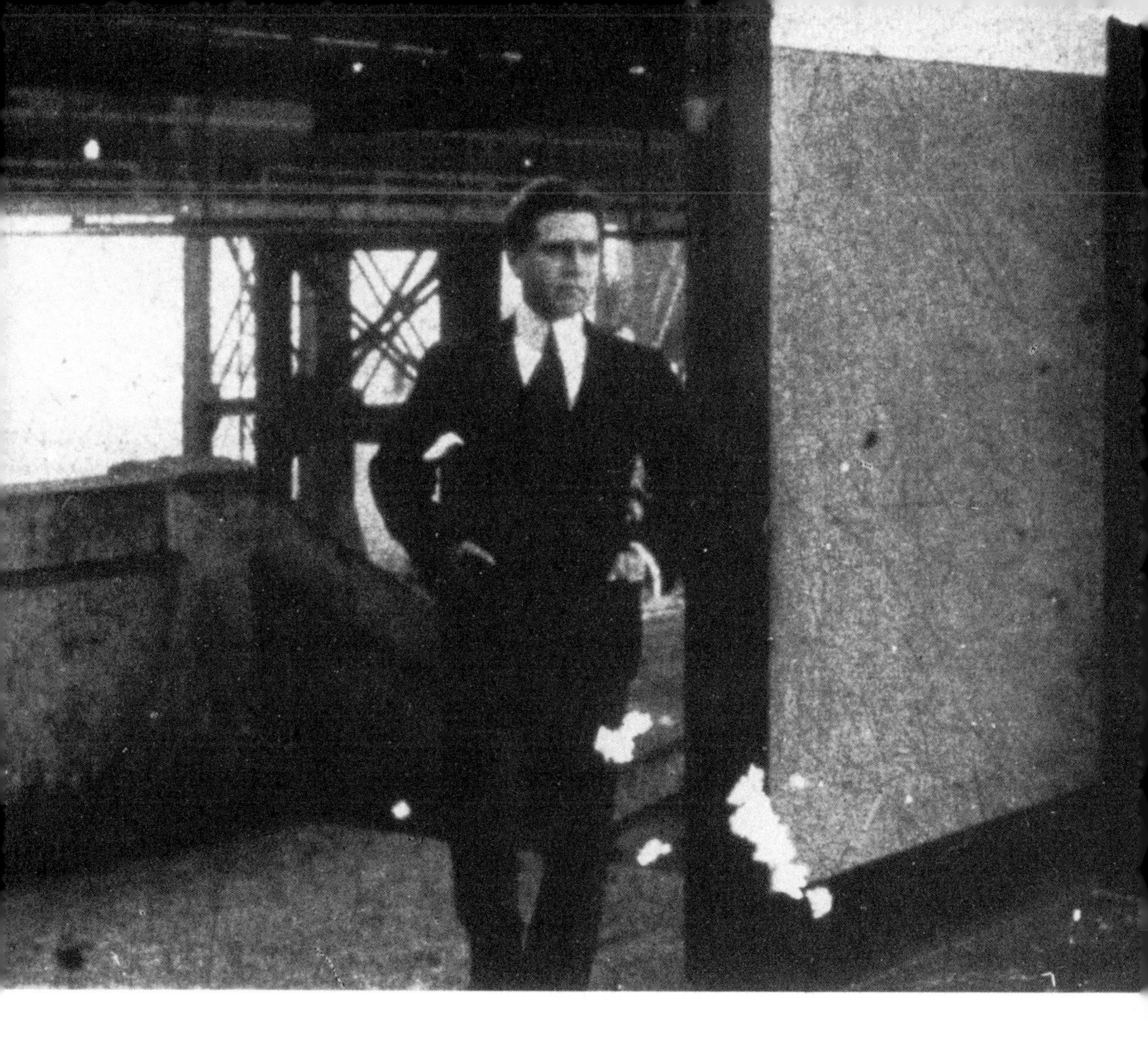

His father drove a truck.

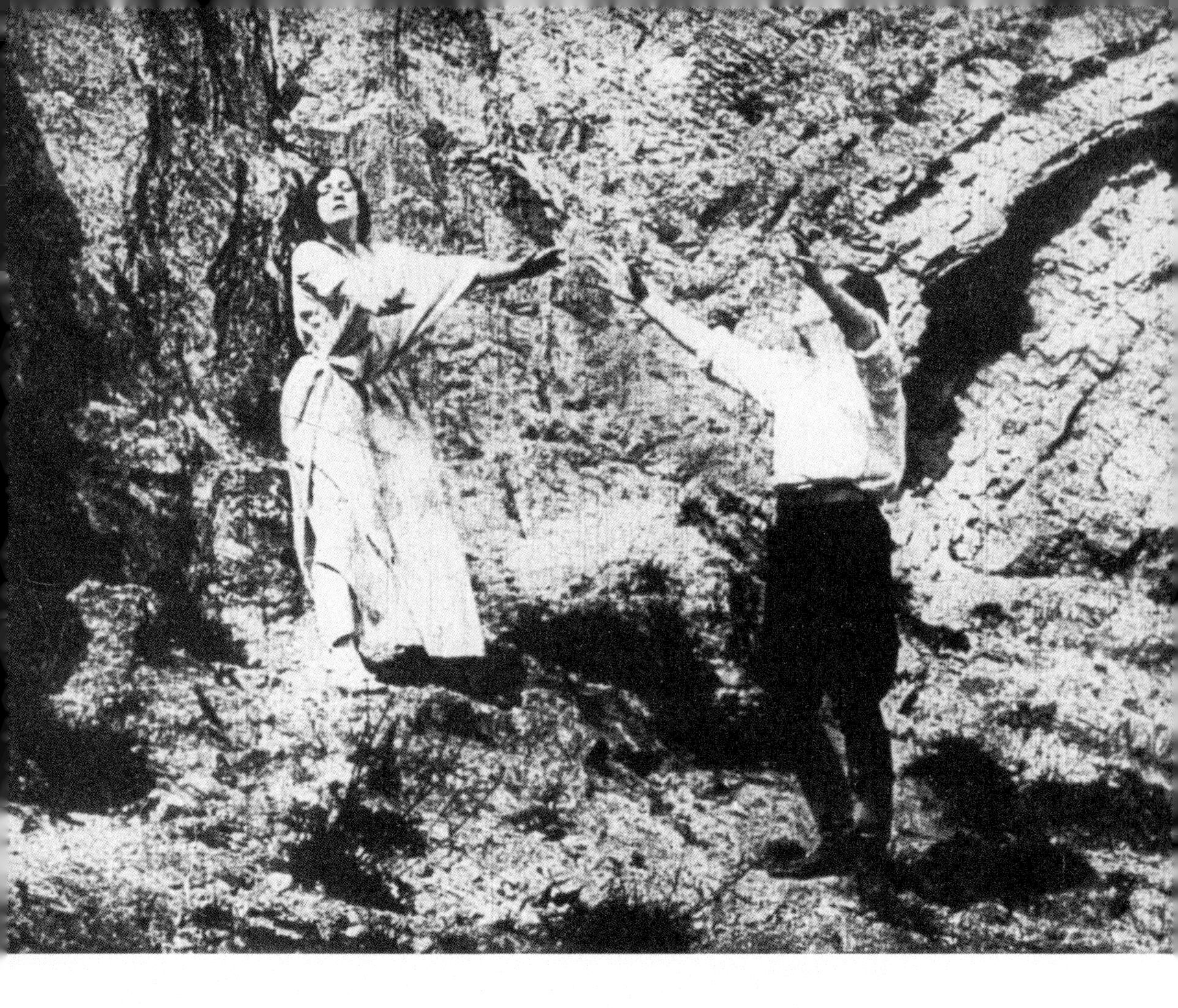

They took walks,

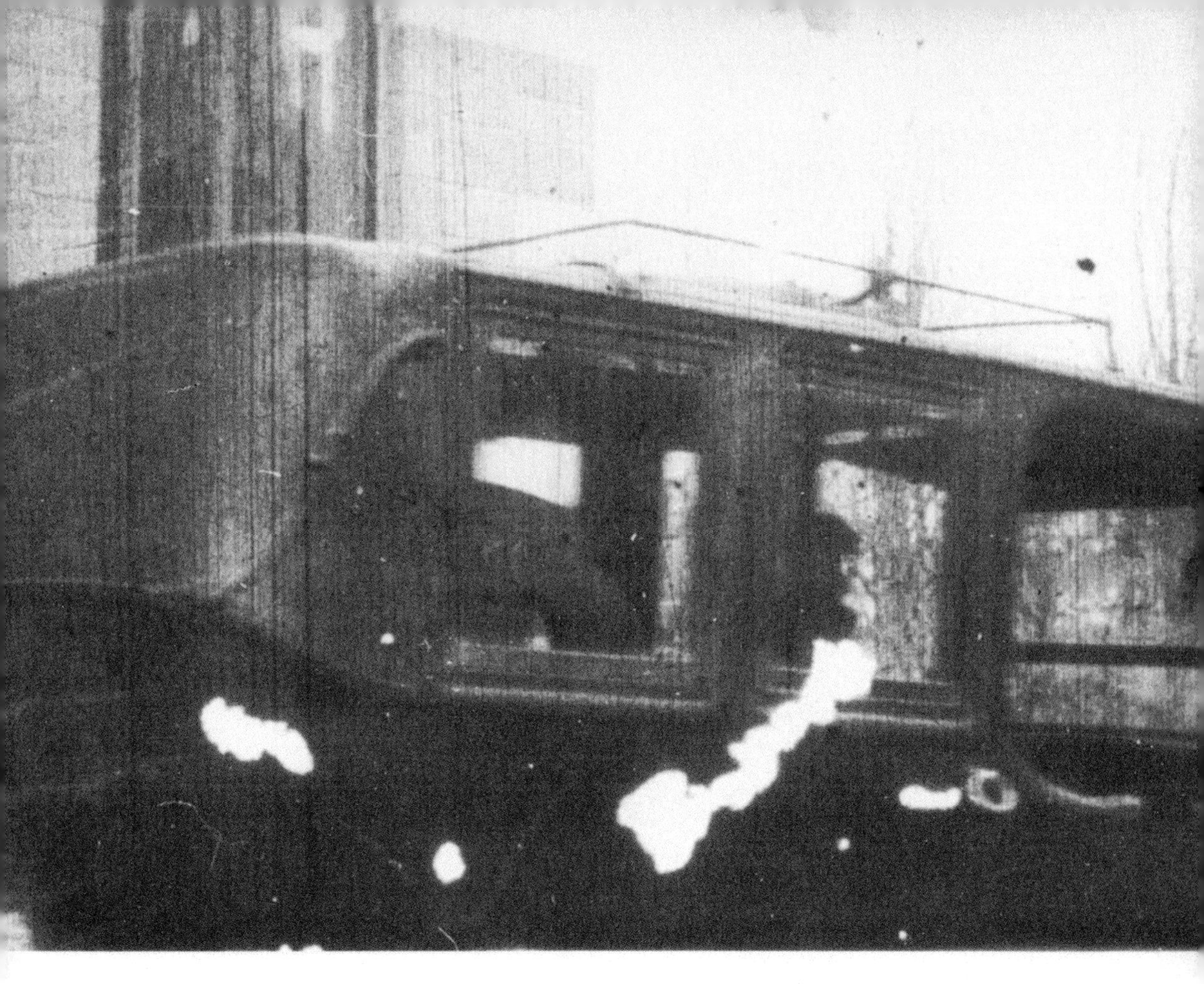

and rides,

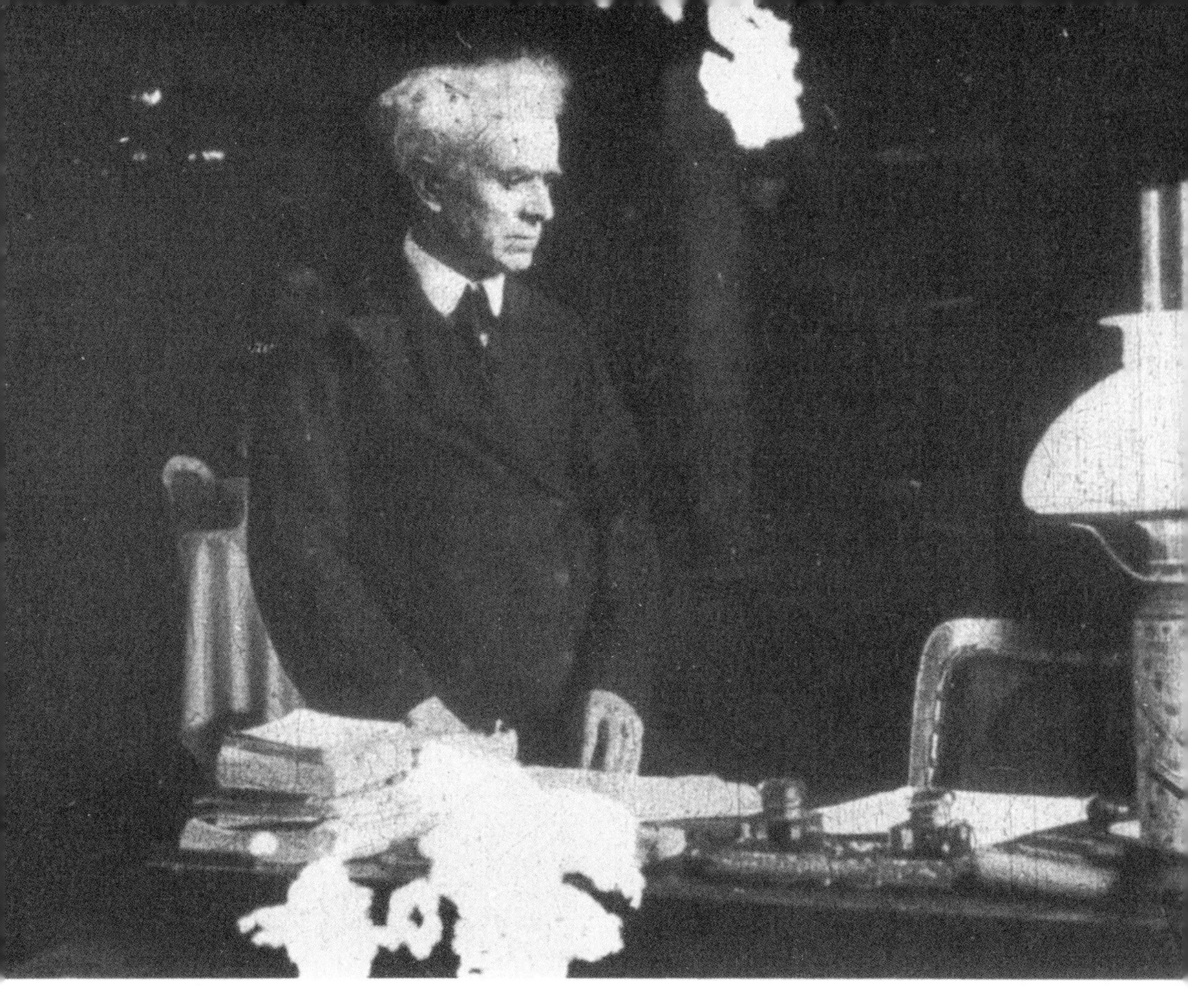

while

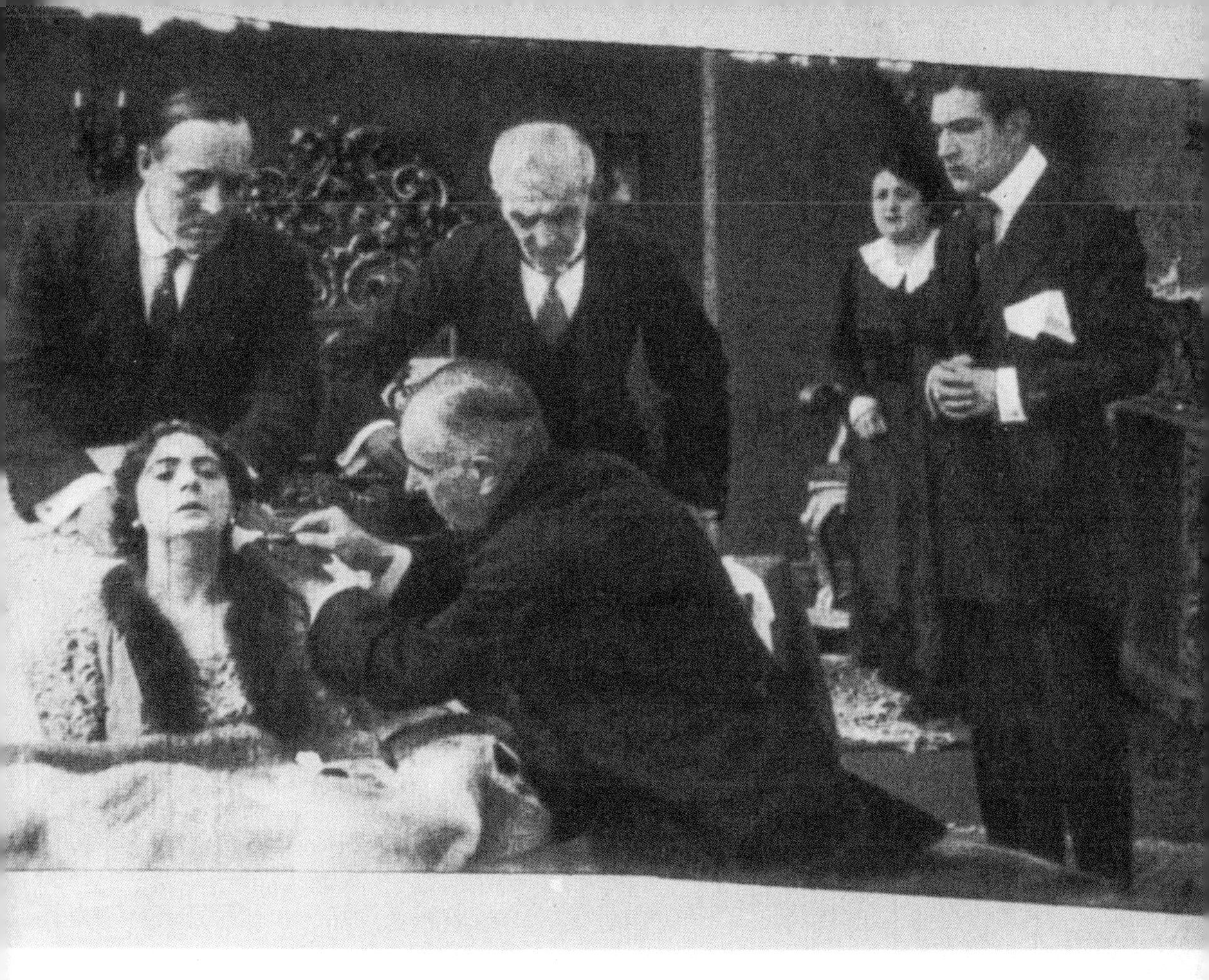

others

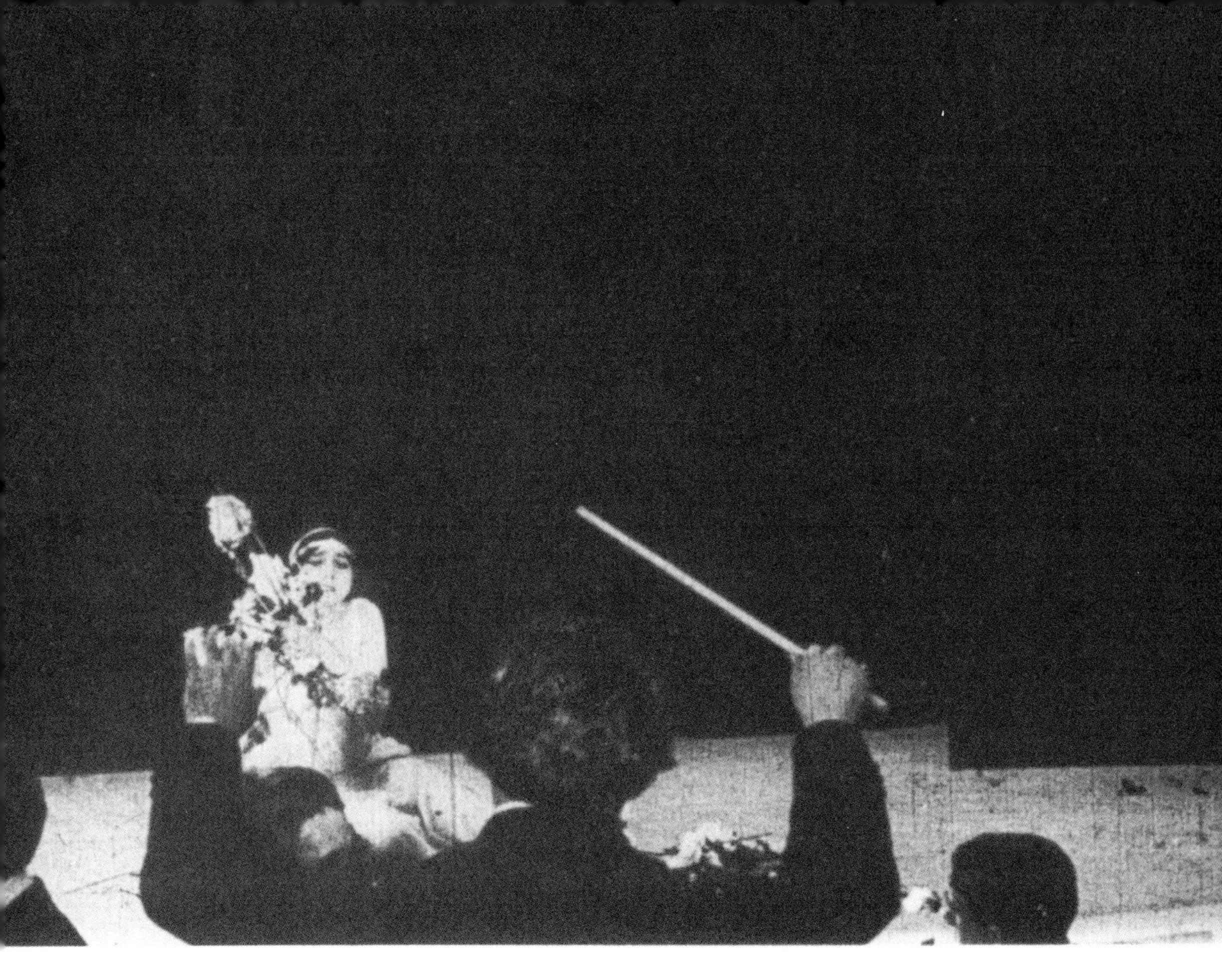

died.

(Untitled)

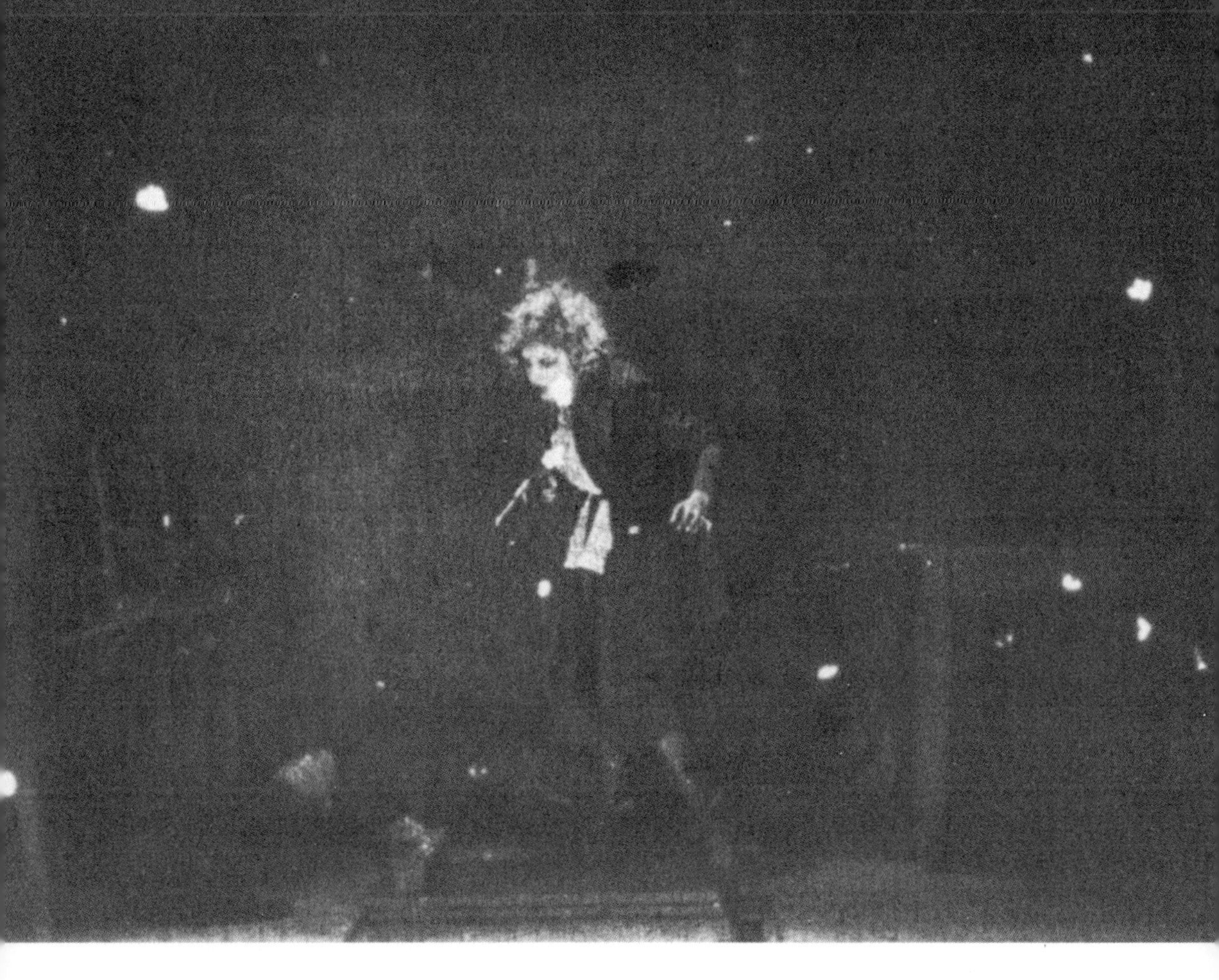

From a diary, she learned
her mother liked the movies.

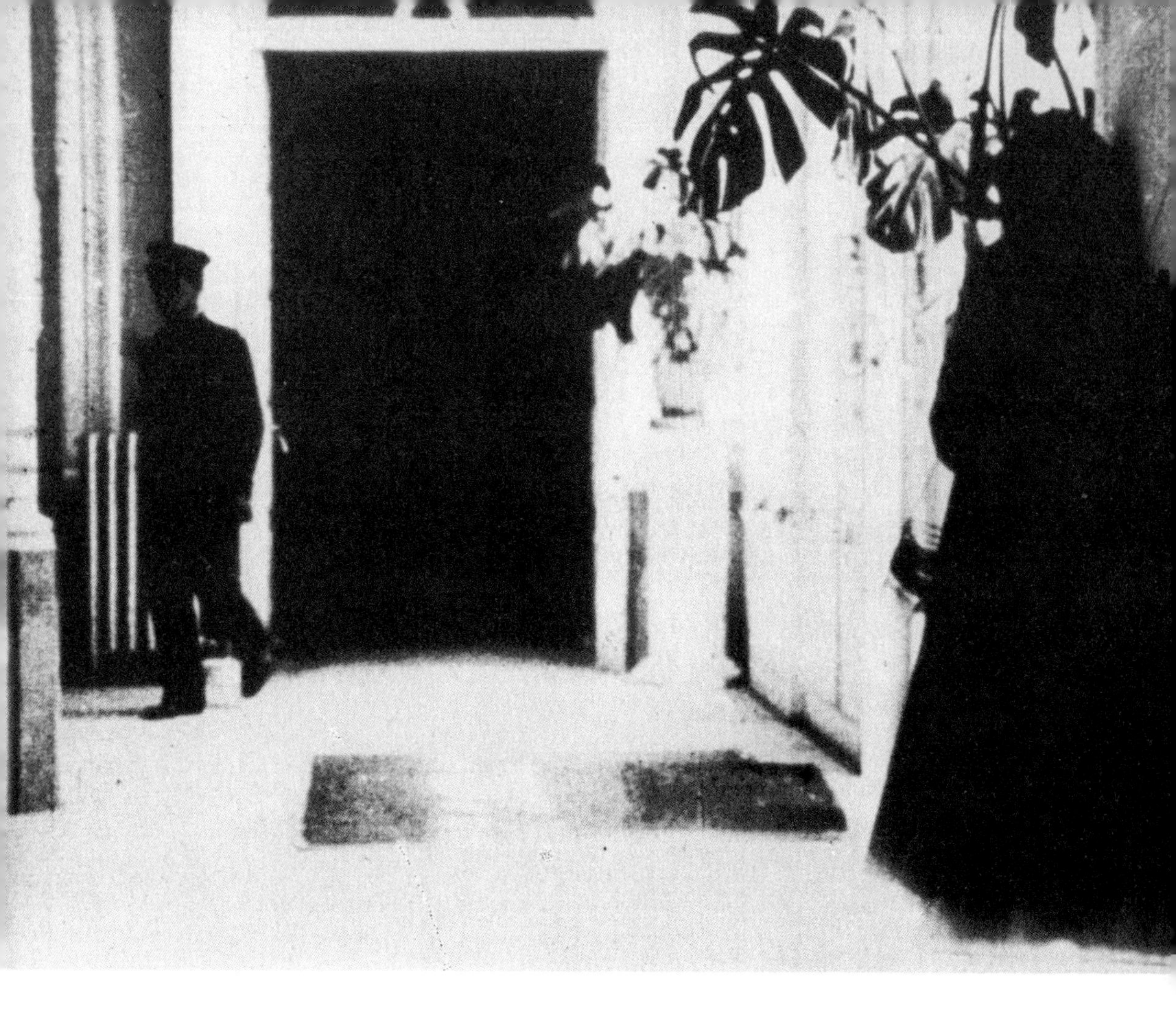

Romantic mysteries with old
actors in black and white

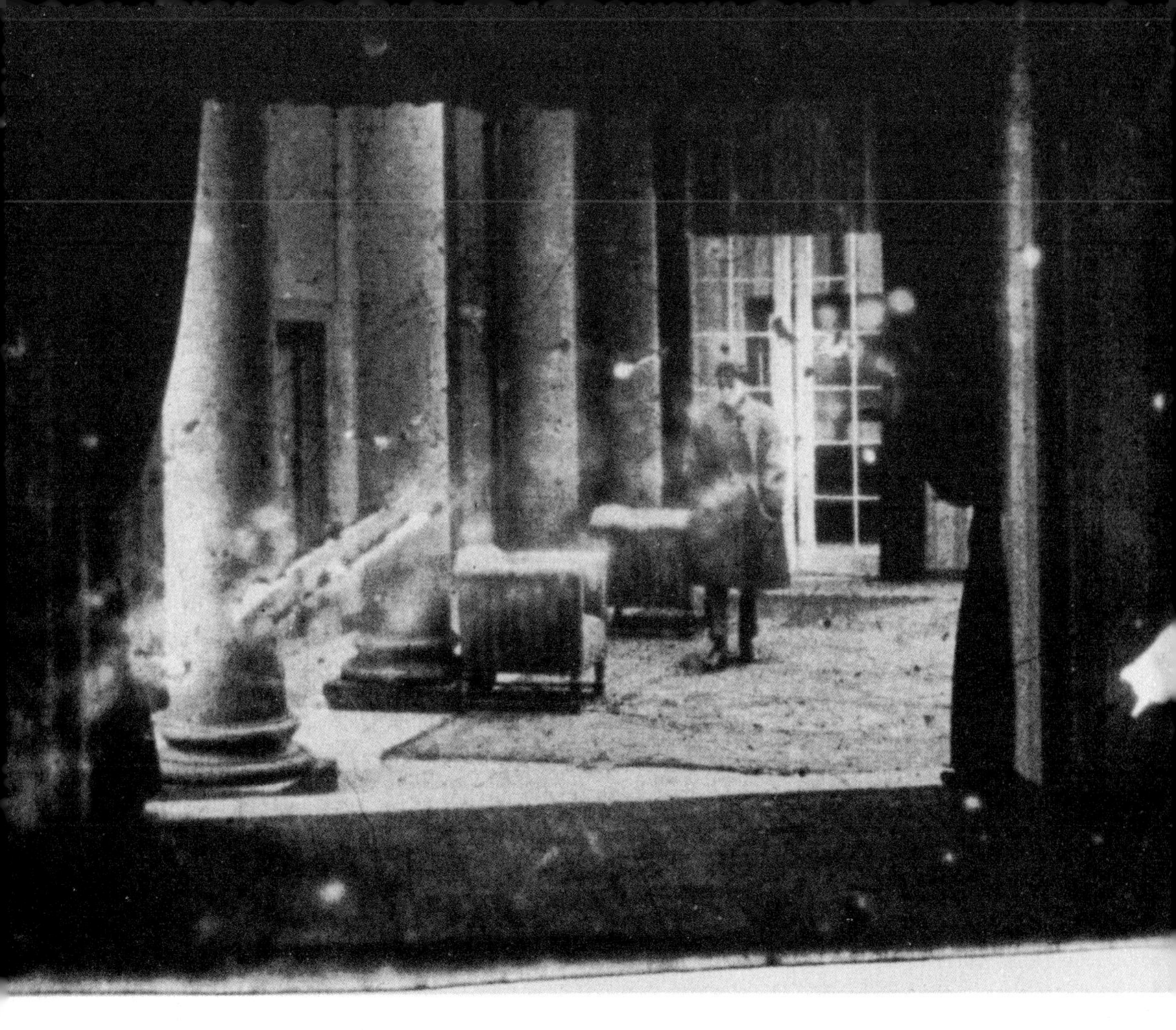

Political drama was
elegant in the 30's.

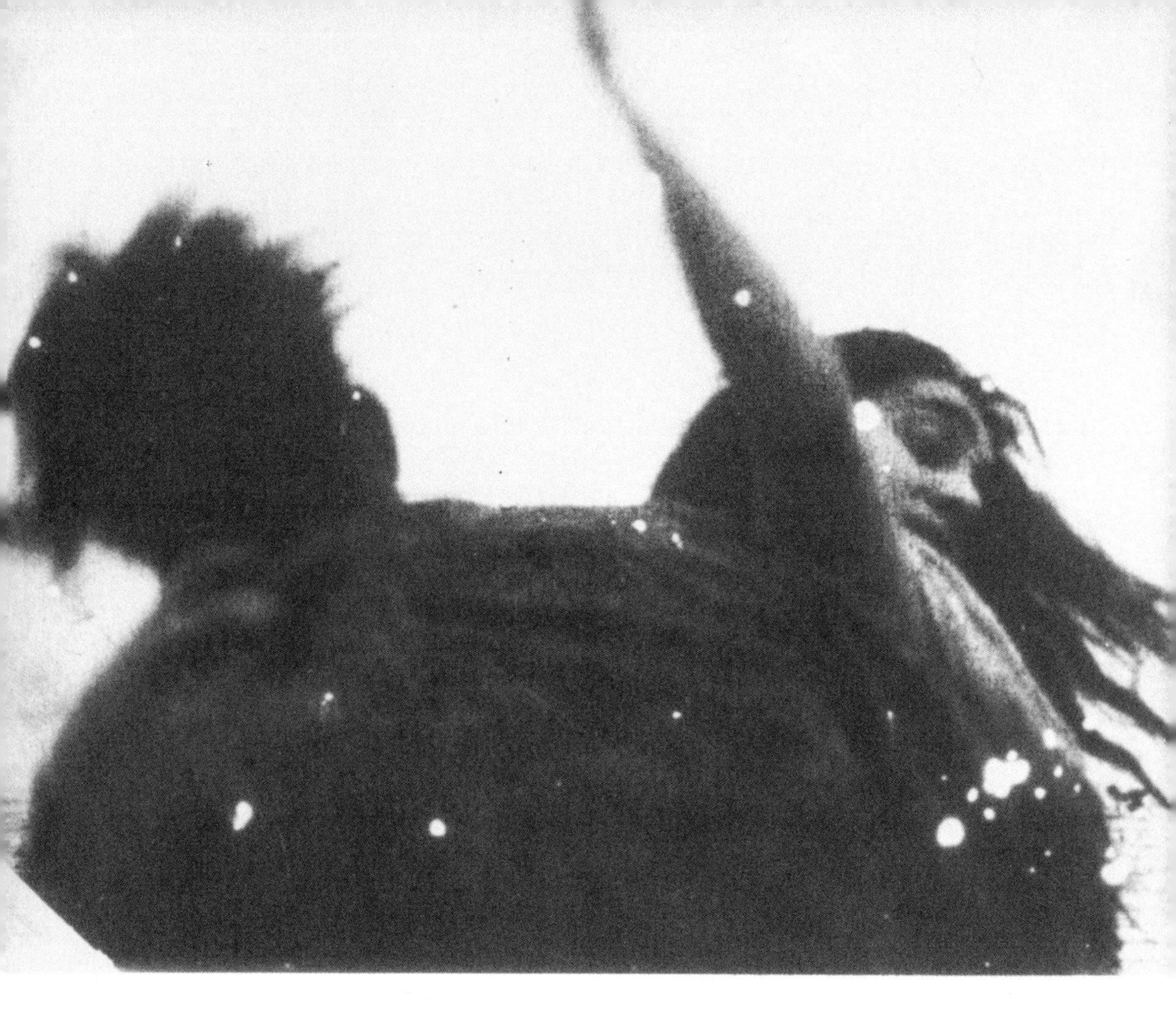

Love stories were best.

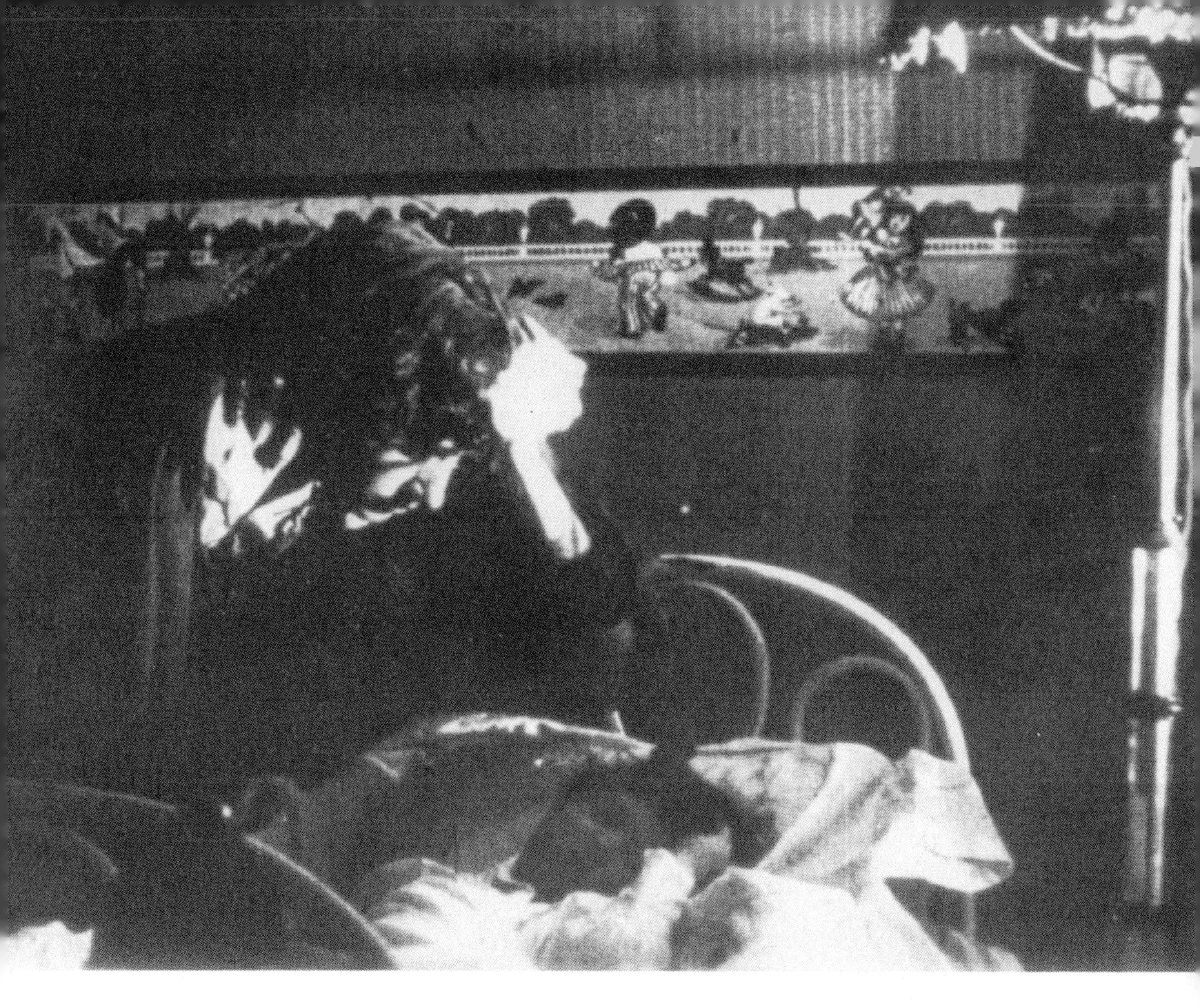

But, mothers were
rarely happy.

La chiave era rima-
sta in suo possesso e...

EDIZIONI ... FILM ROM...

(untitled)

... losing all let her forget

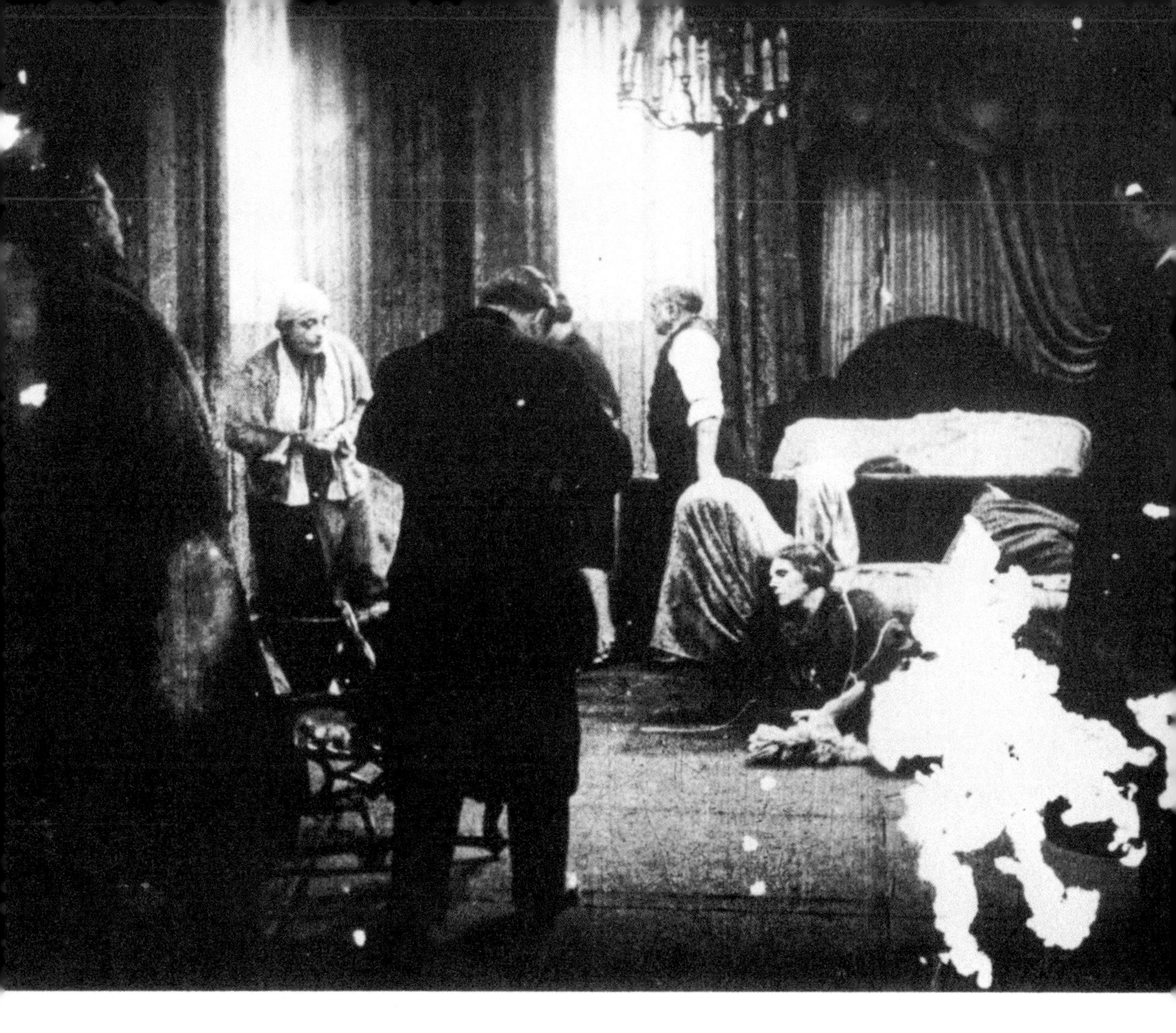

She never liked her homes;
losing all let her forget.

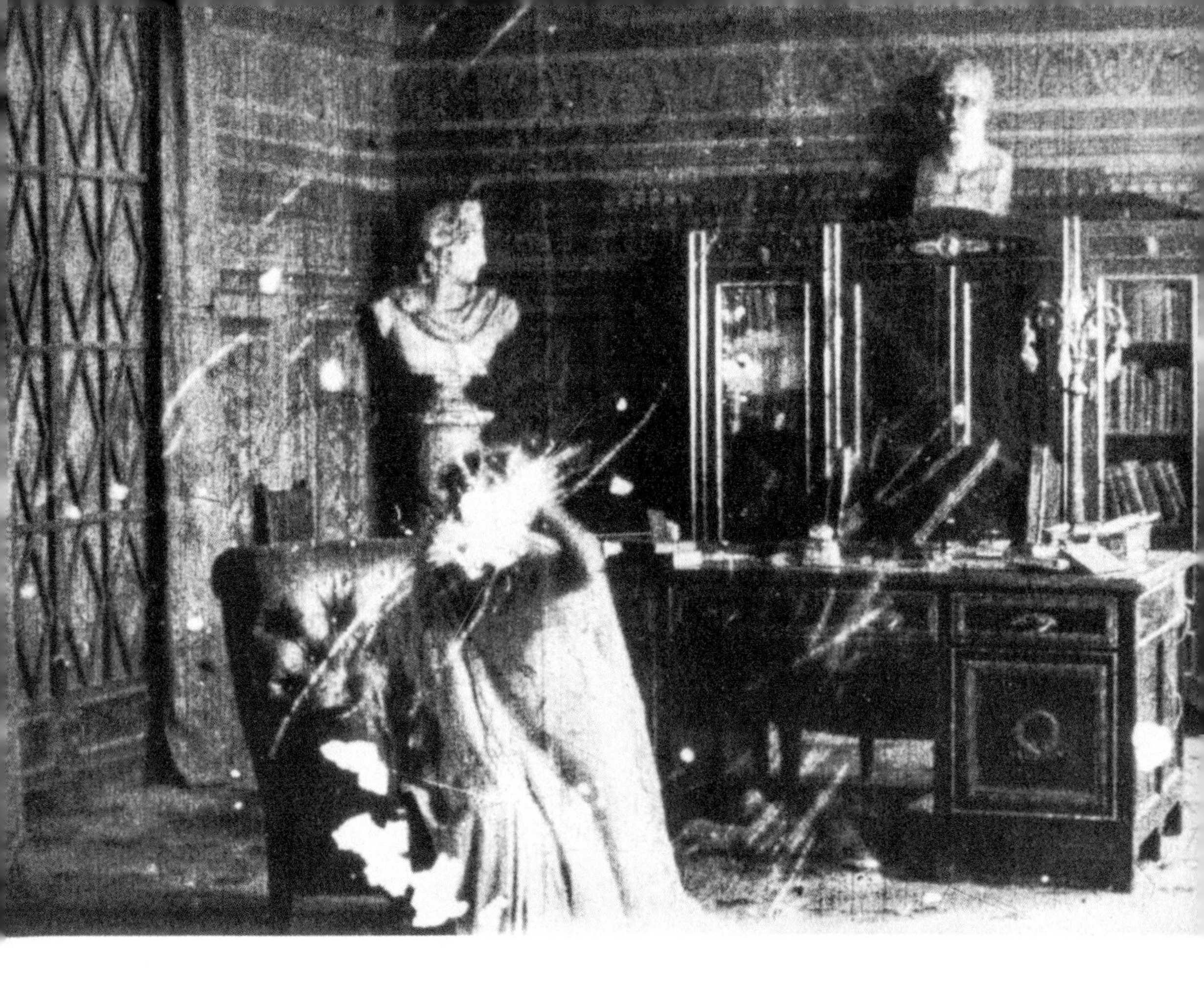

They were all old-rich
southern, and she the
madest.

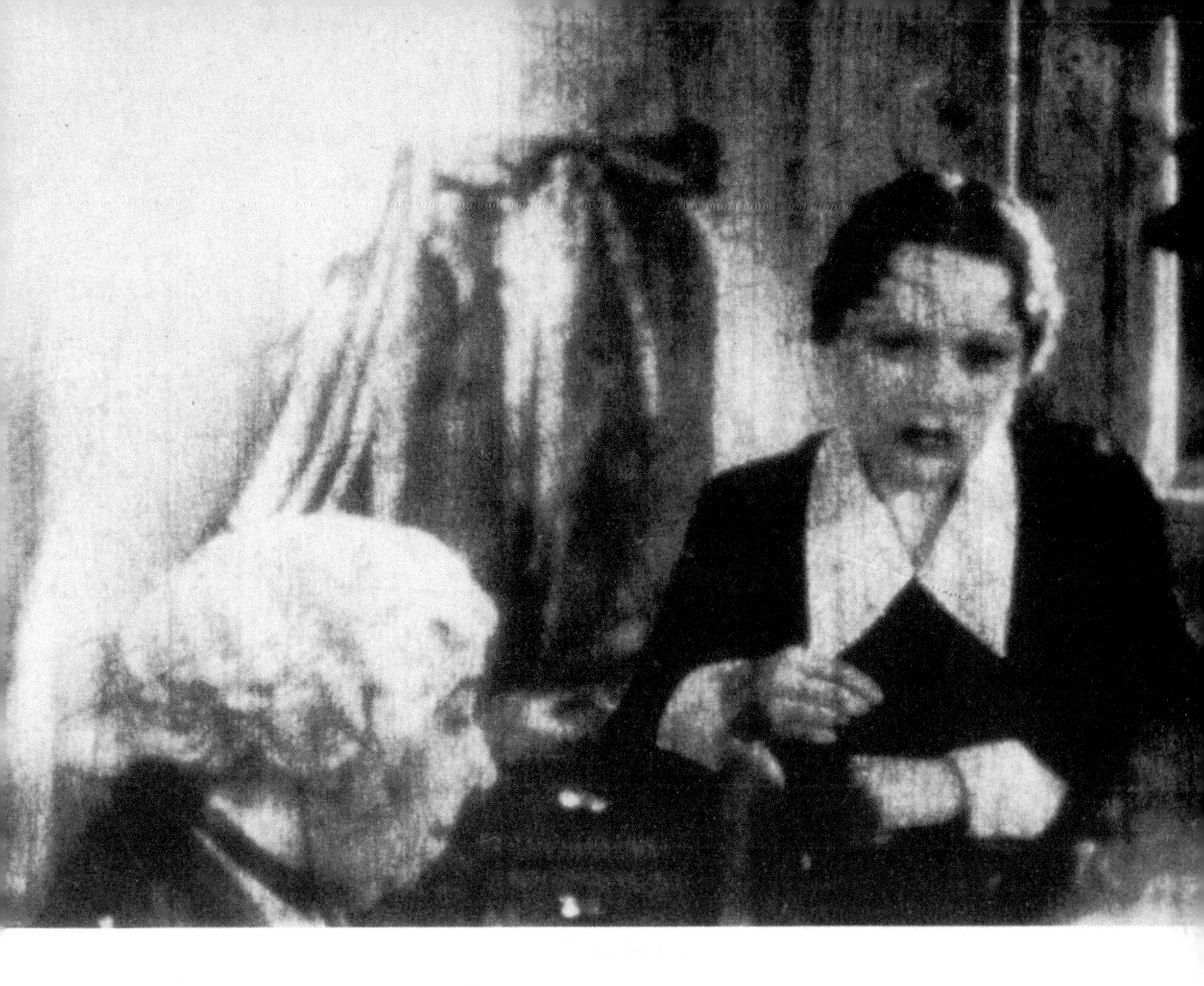

Her mother quoted the Bible,
and guests came from Europe
for sittings.

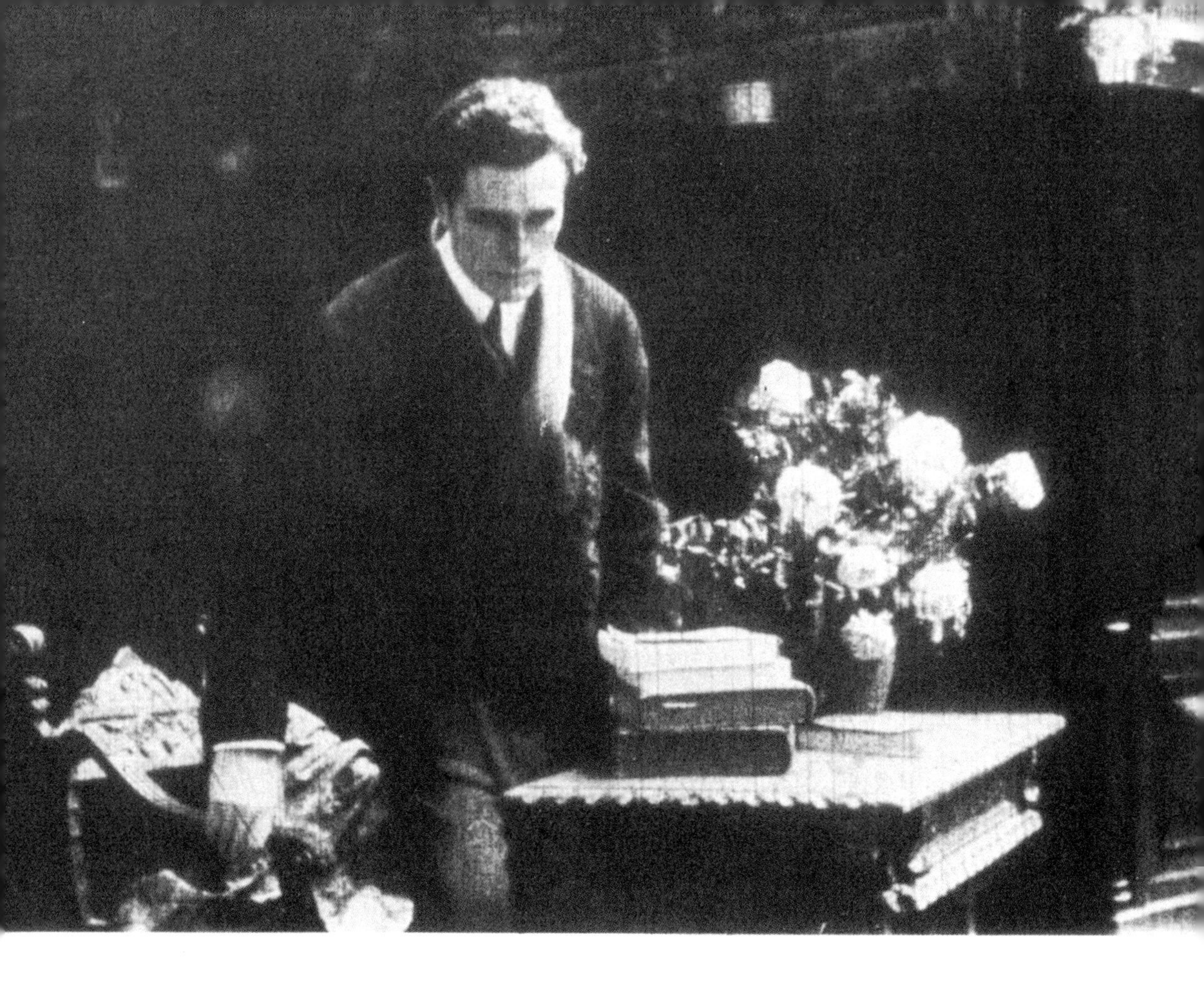

Her fifth husband was a
carpenter who prefered to be
nude on the third floor stairs,

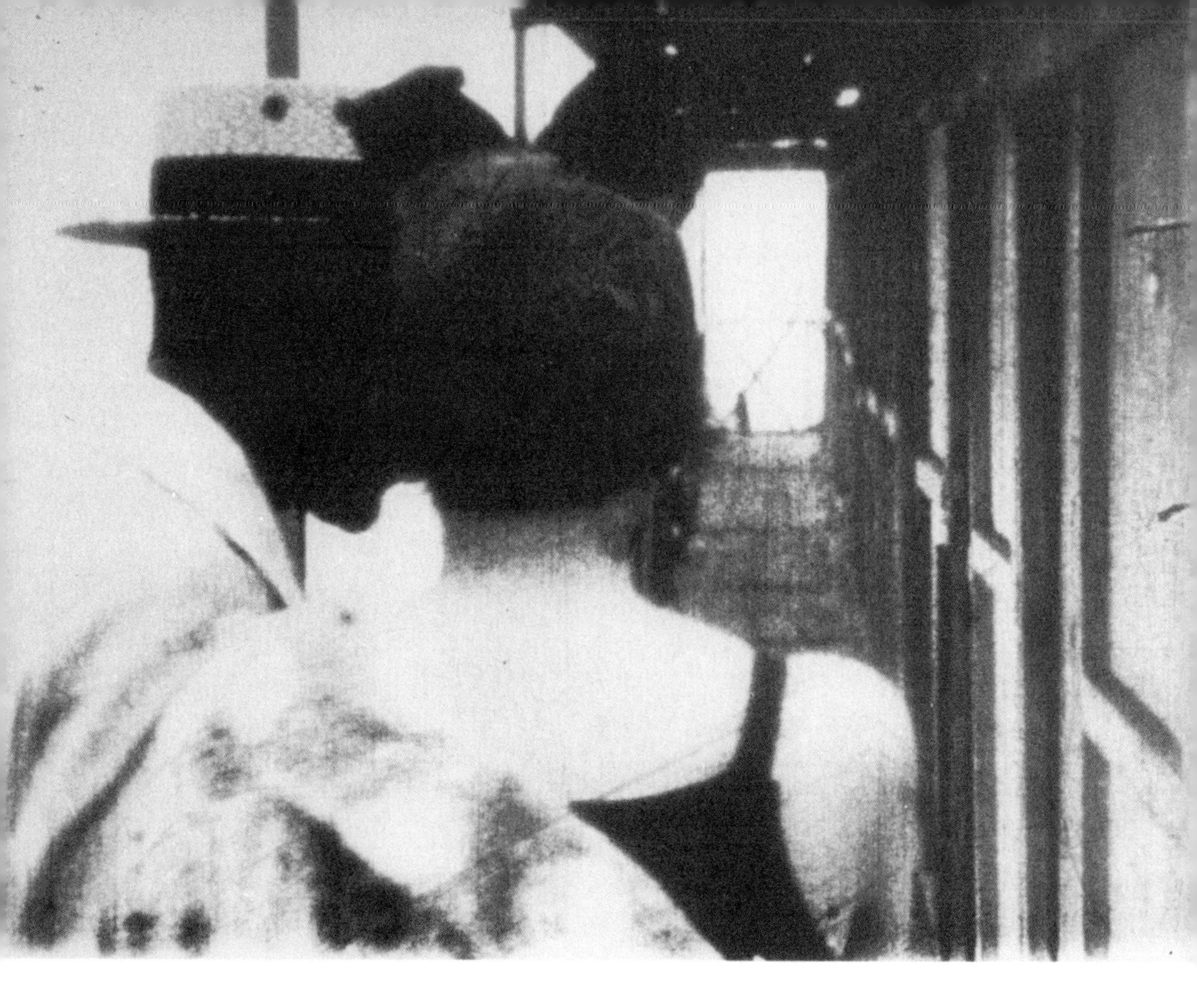

The children were elegant
and married late.

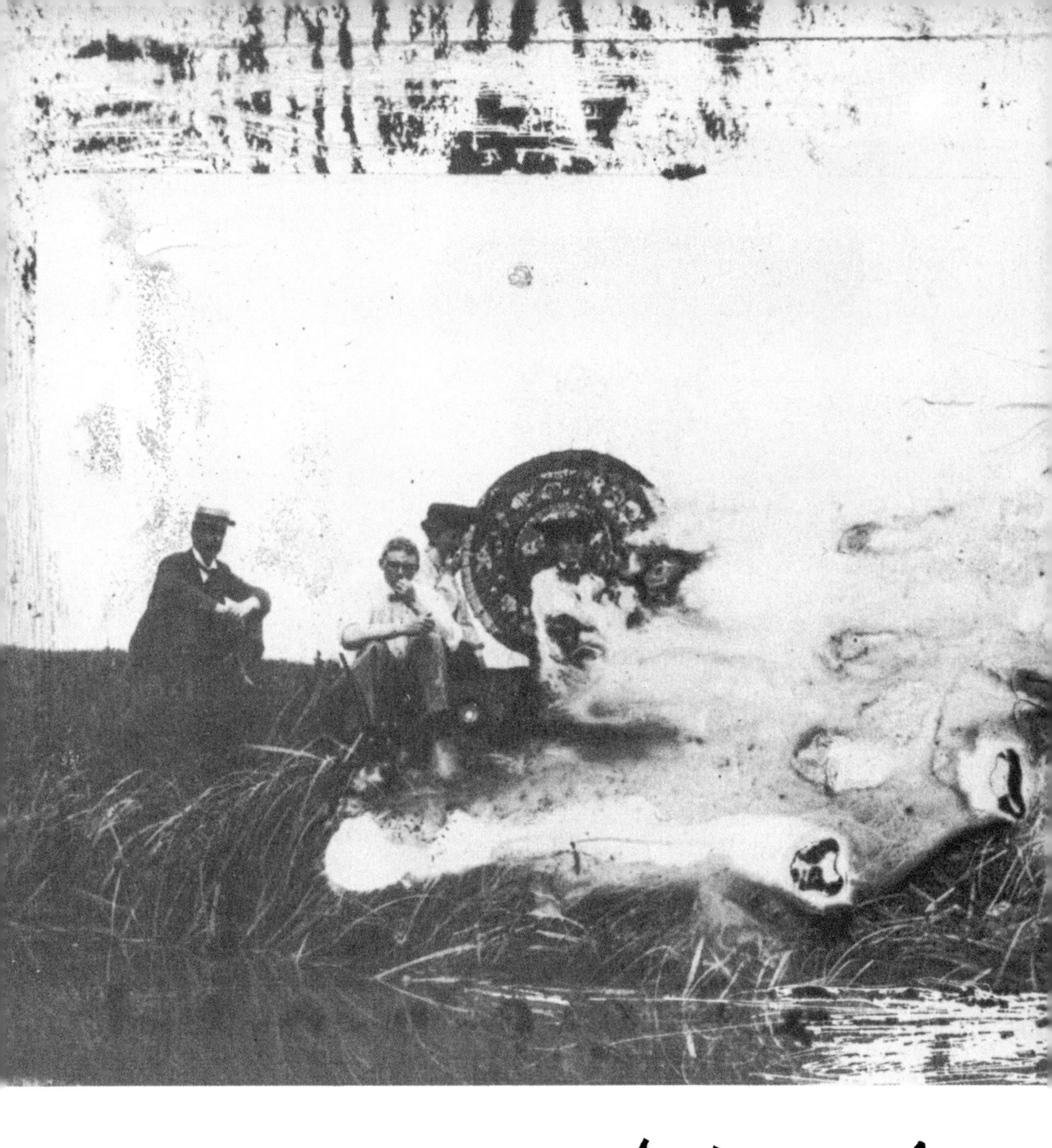

Blood clots reached her lung.
Others had removed both legs,

He was romantic

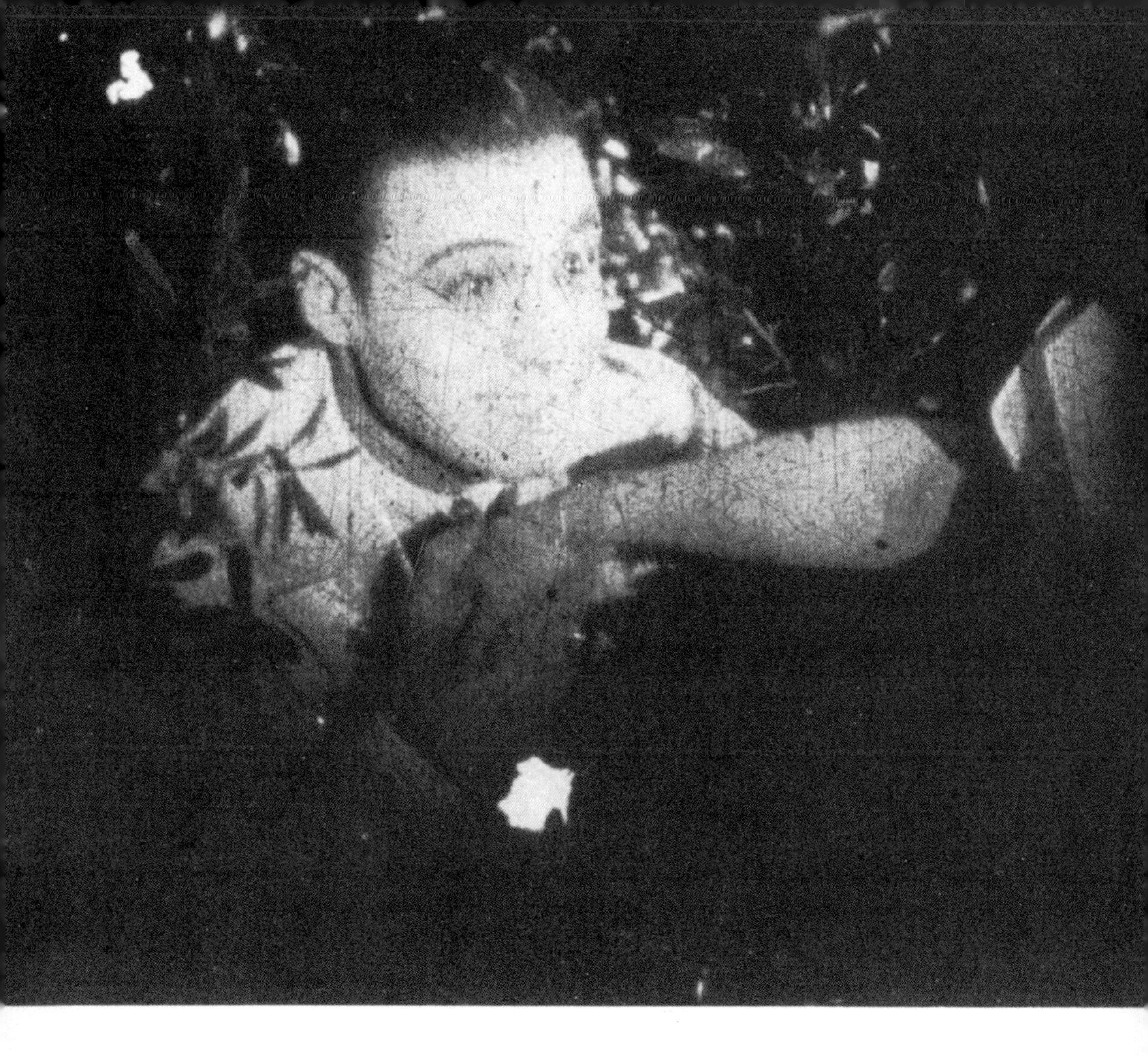

He was romantic
to many ladies,

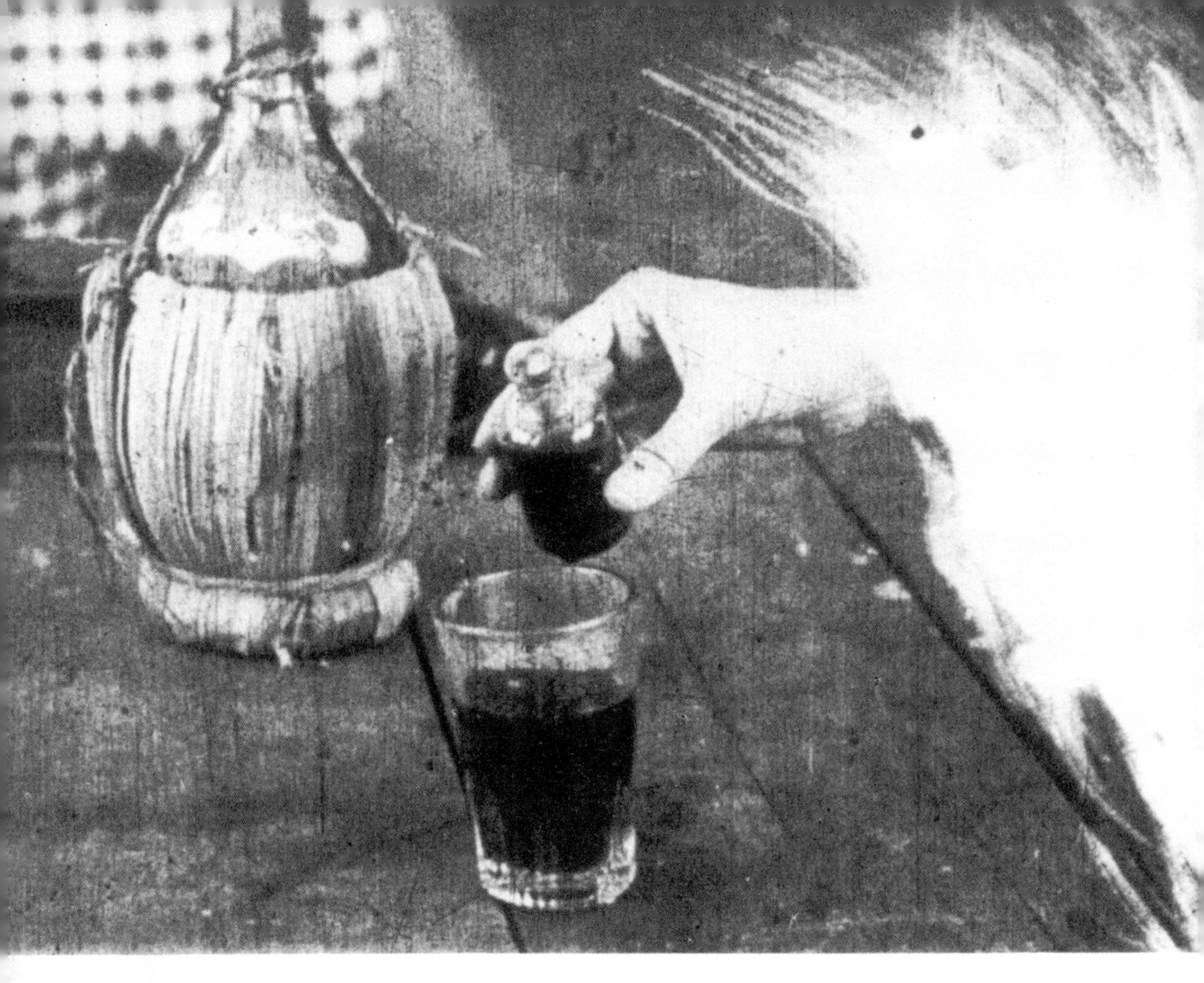

drank a lot,

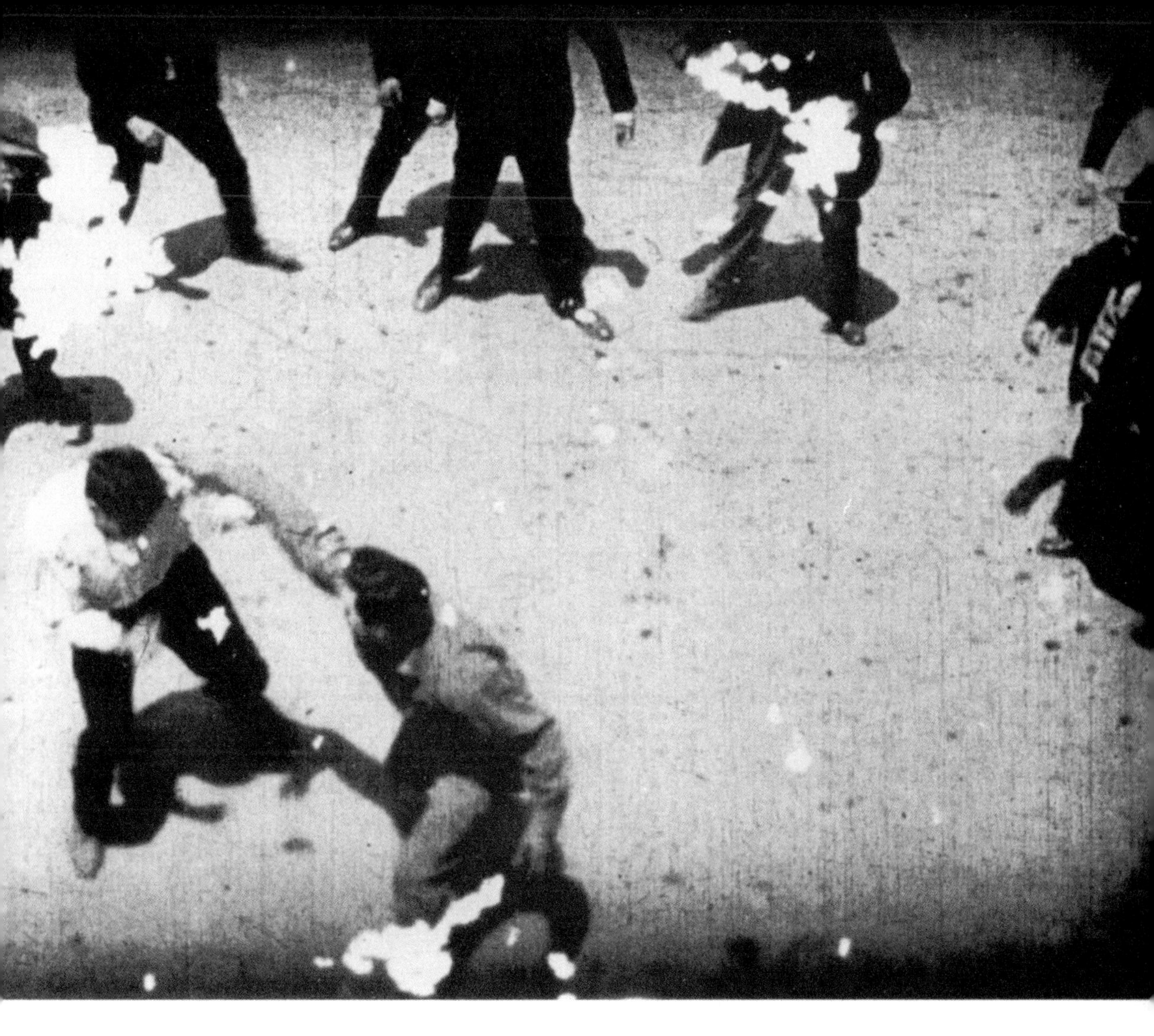

fought together
with workers,

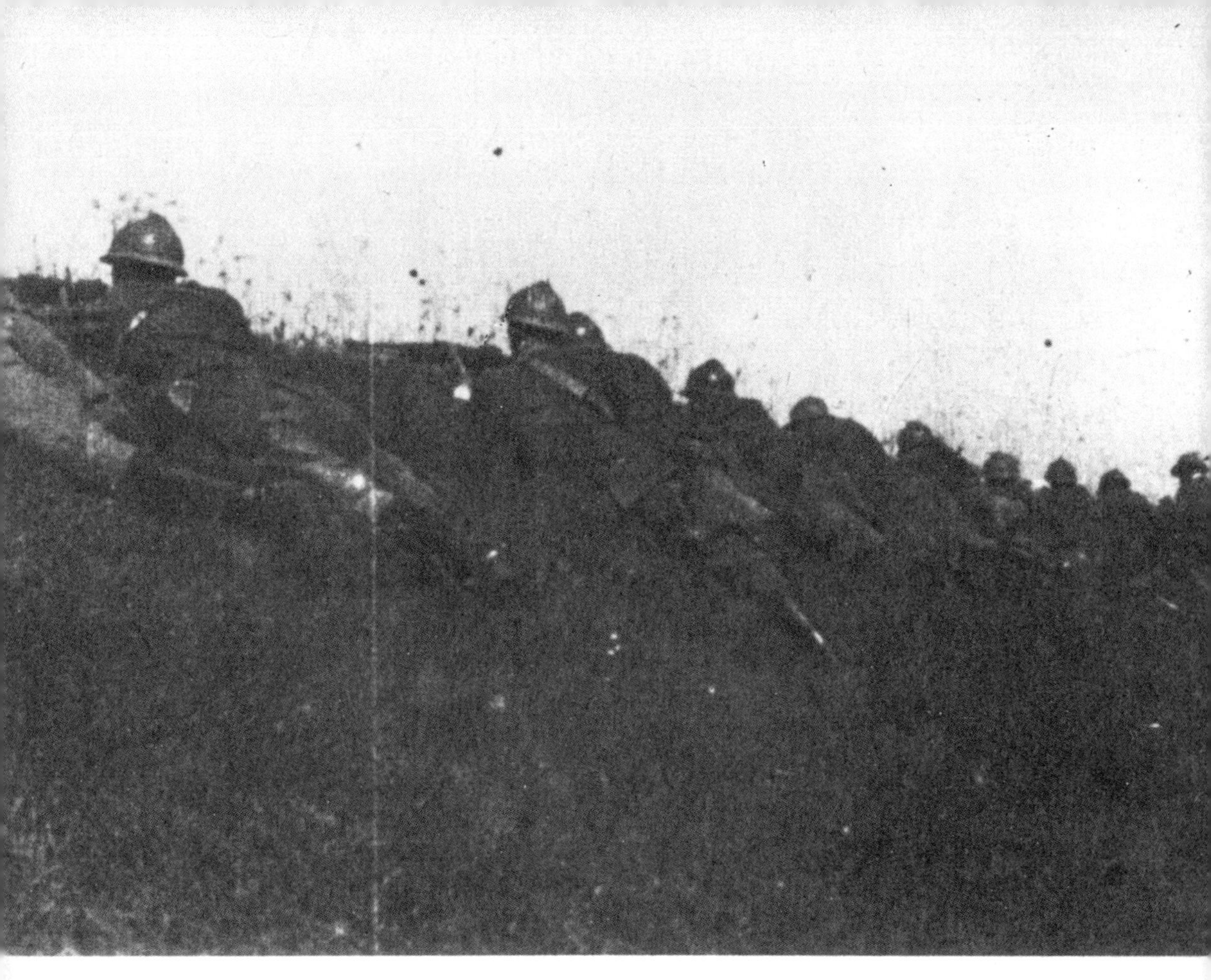

soldiers,

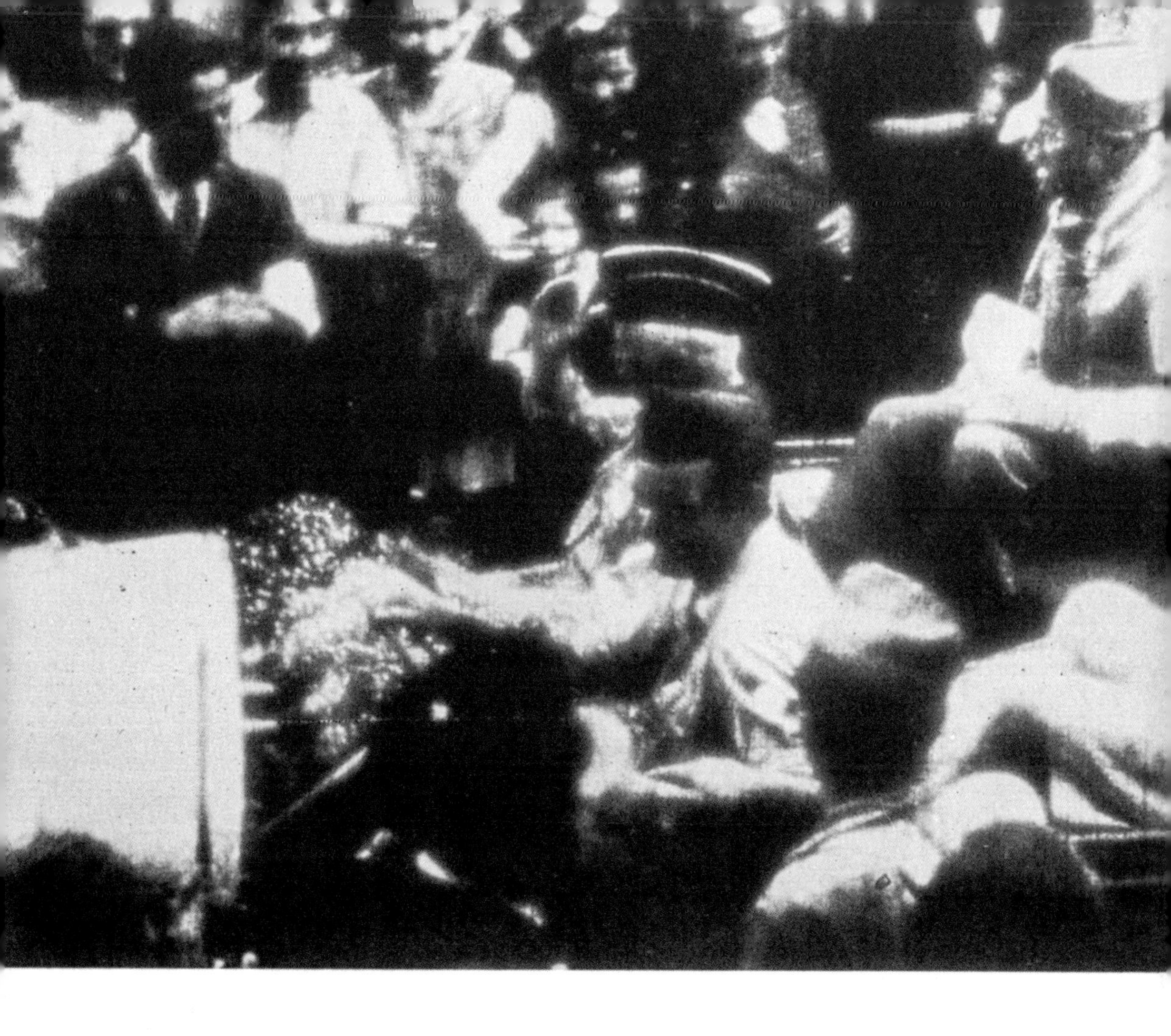

and watched the
generals drive by later.

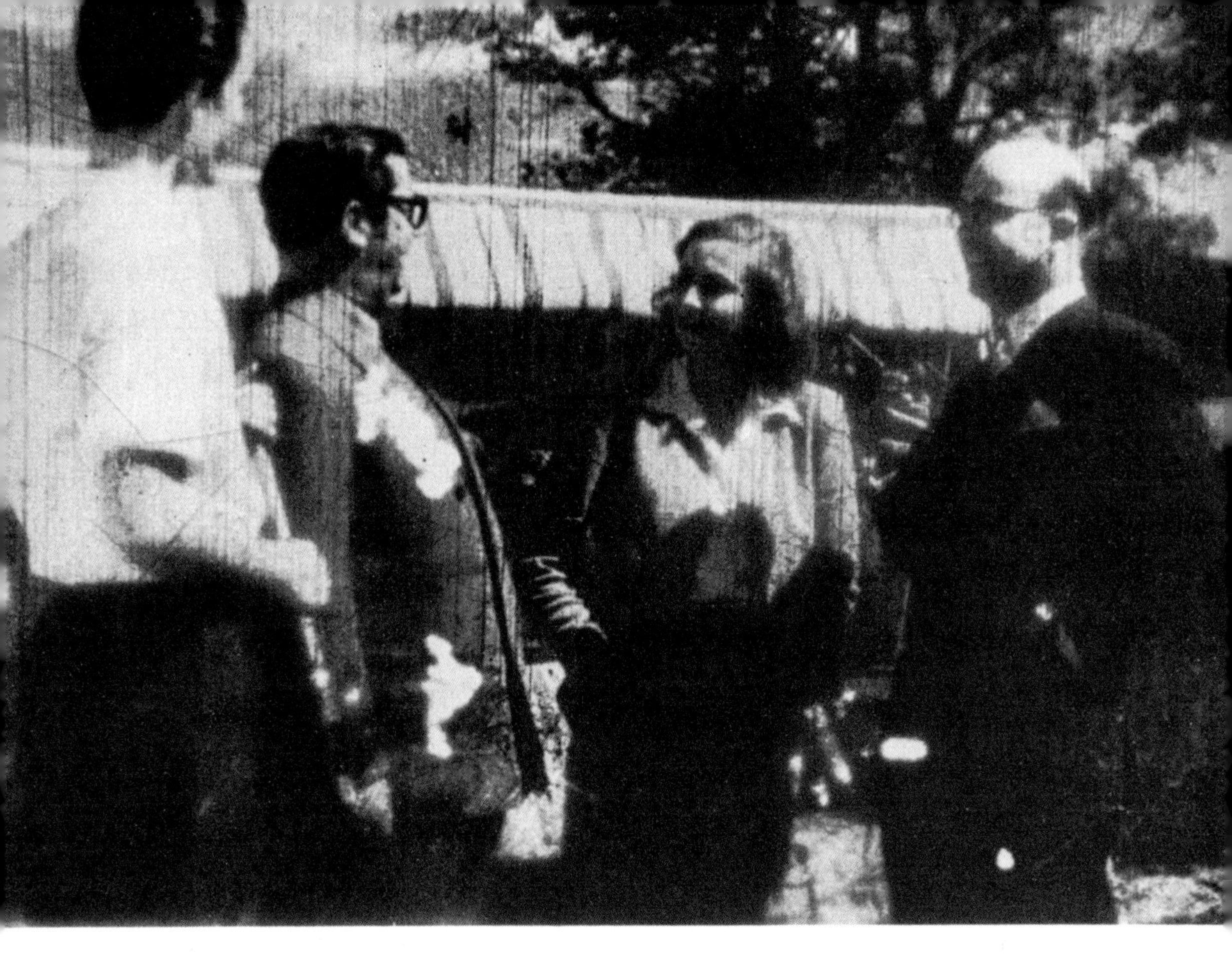

America had won the war

... up in the air

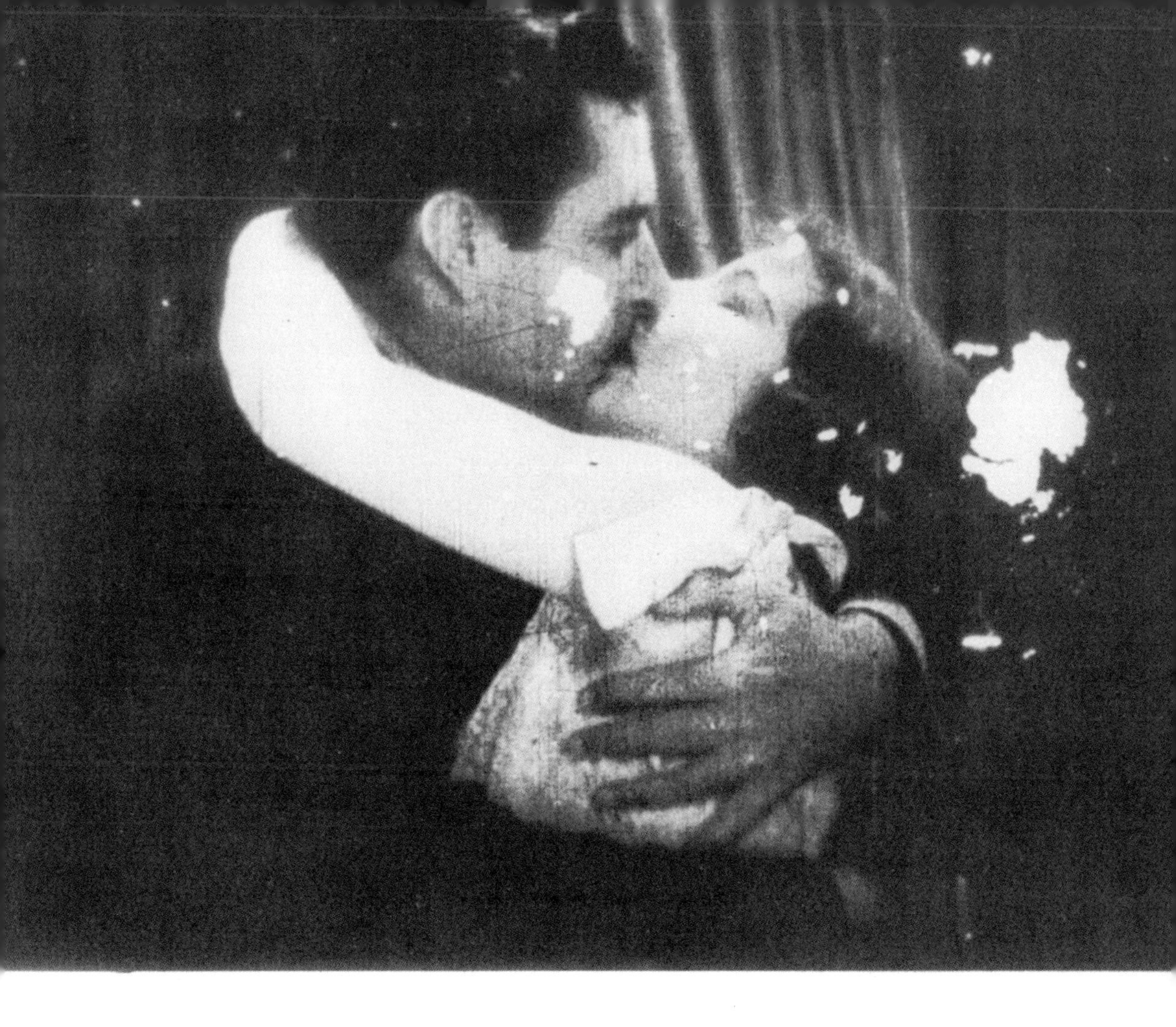

She met a Greek mechanic
while looking for a Porsche,

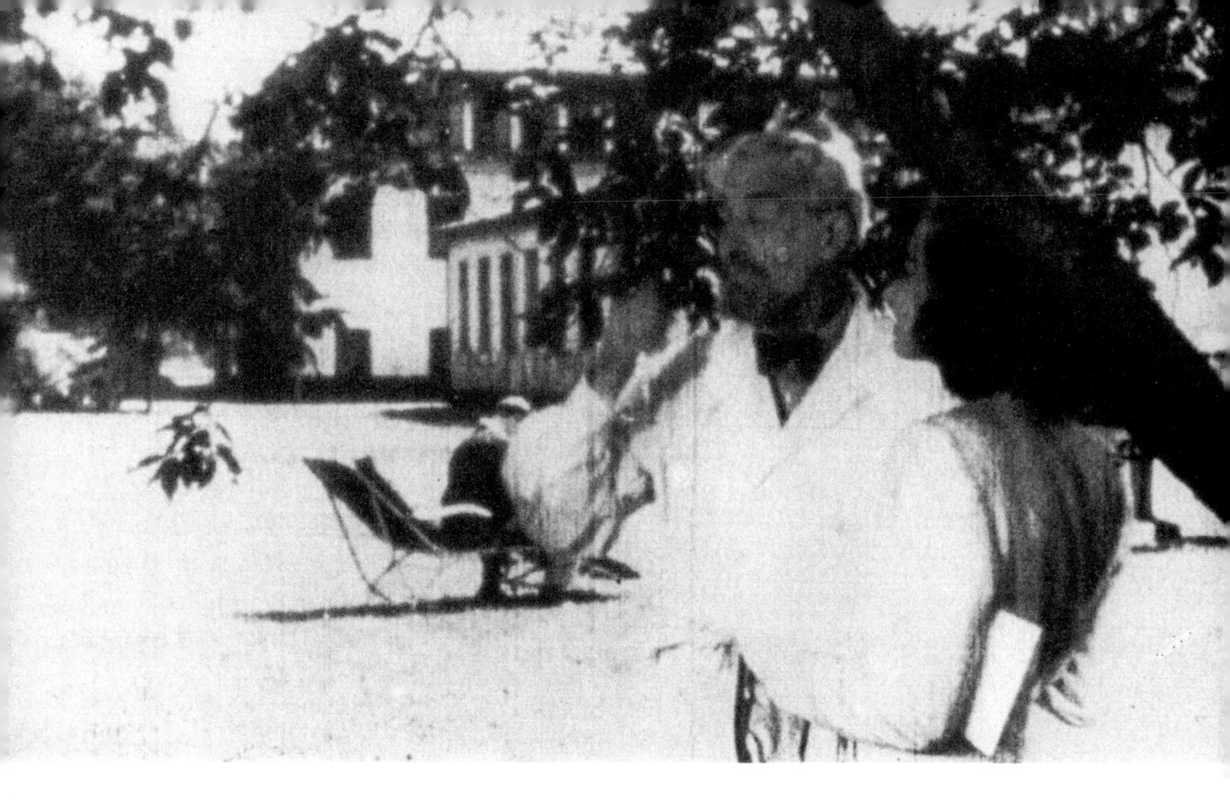

Before and after, an astro-physicist lived in an elevator building near campus.

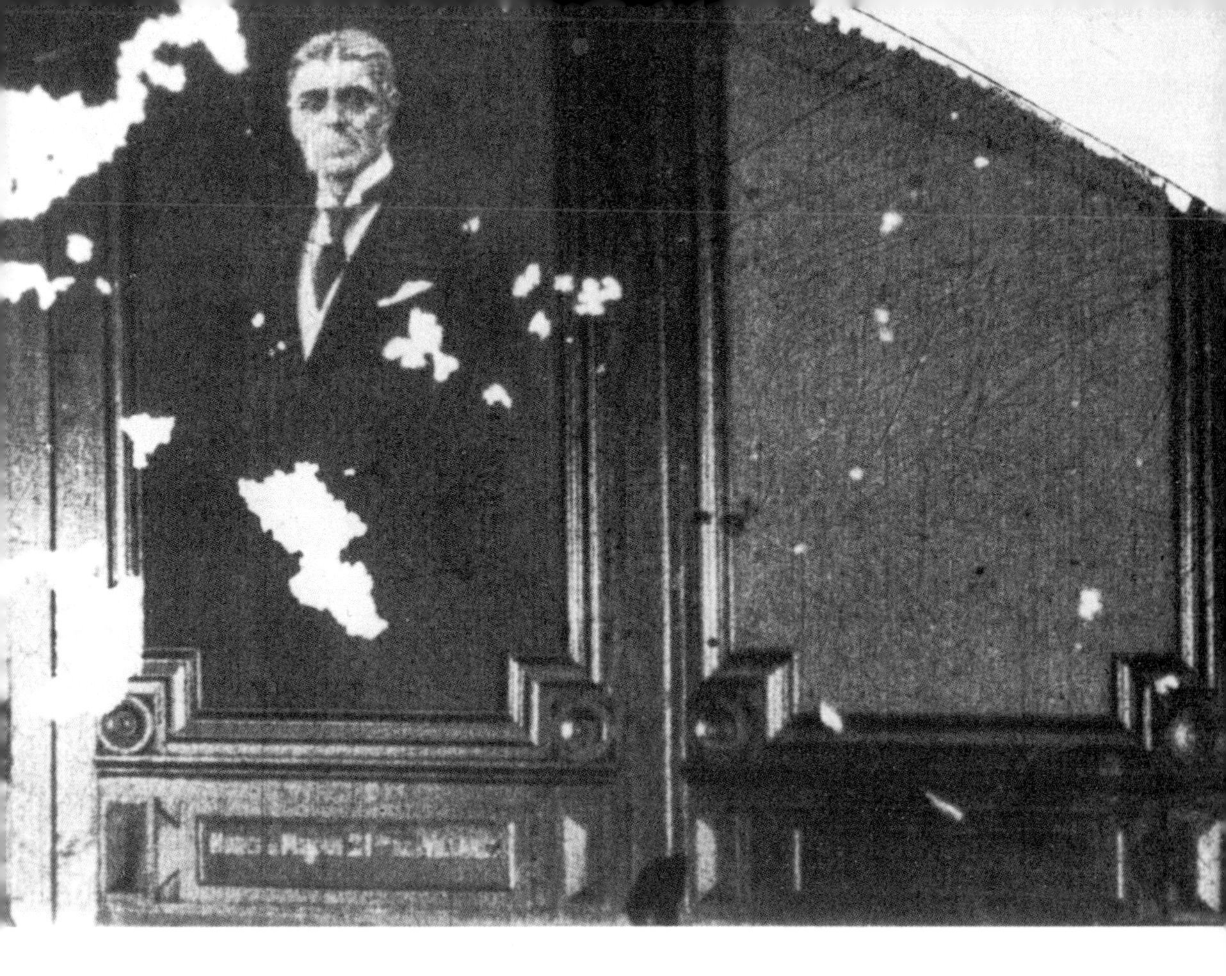

A spanish revolutionary economist
introduced her to the only
son of a dead english Lord
aviator hero.

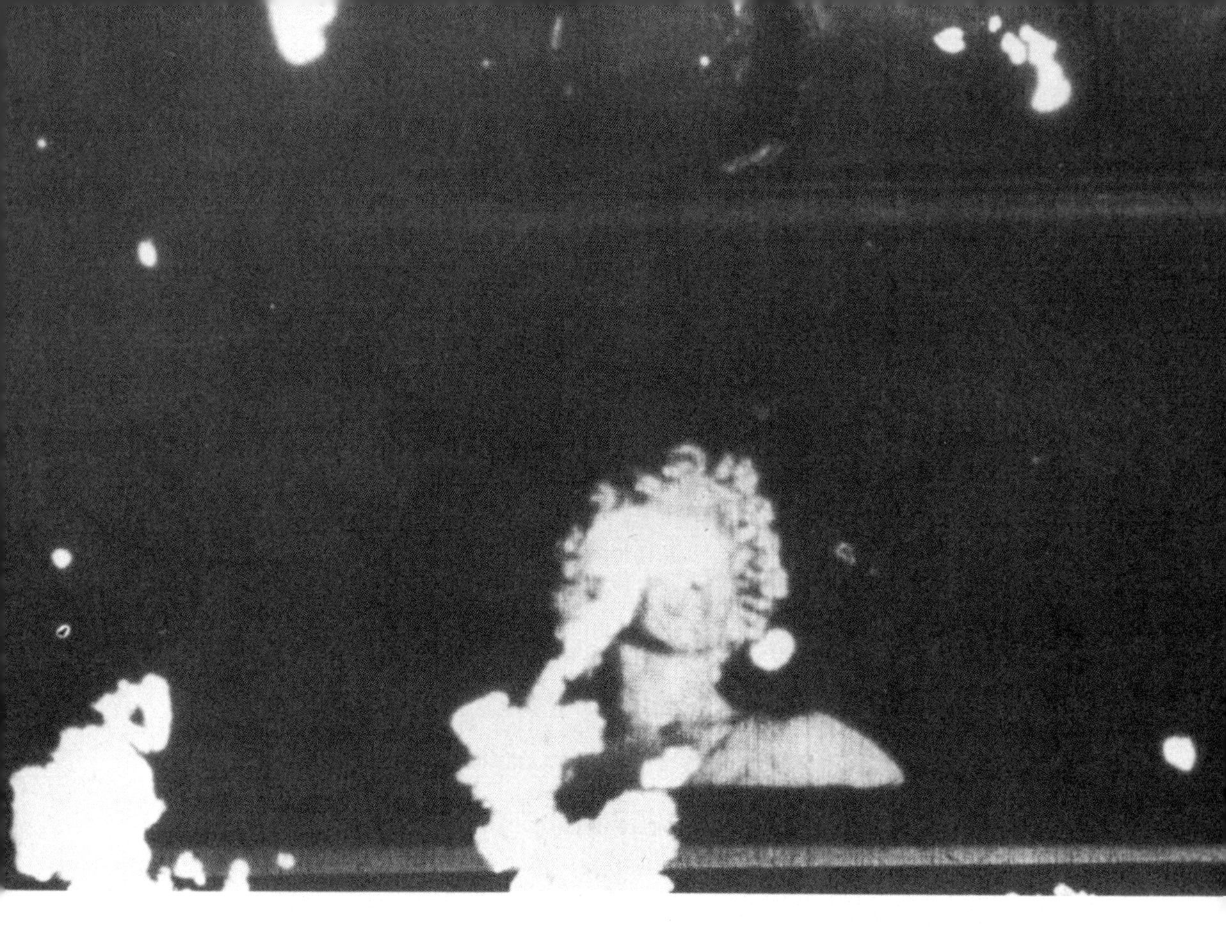

In N.Y. an Ad. poet in decline
introduced her to remarkable
men.

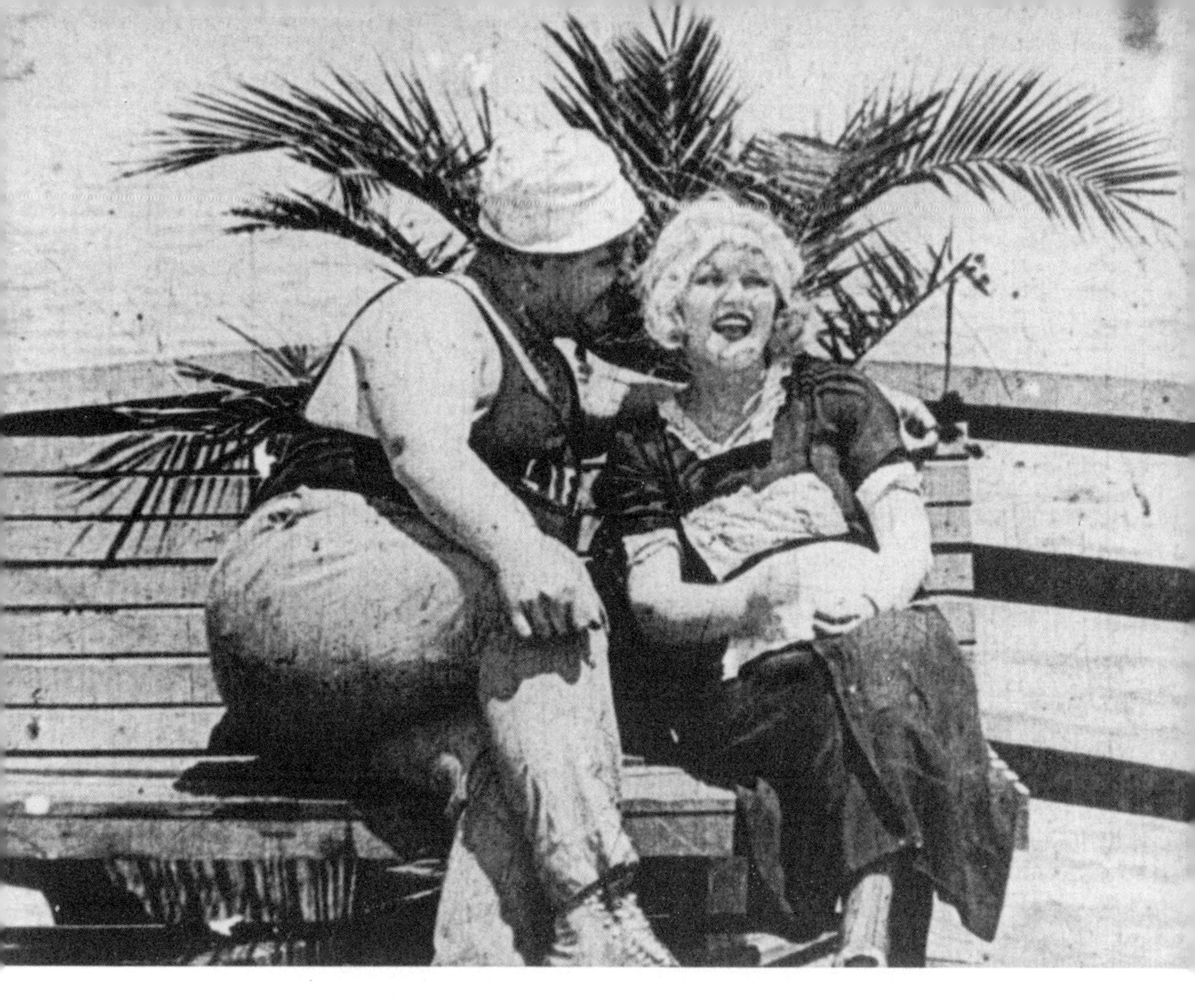

But, after the revolution,

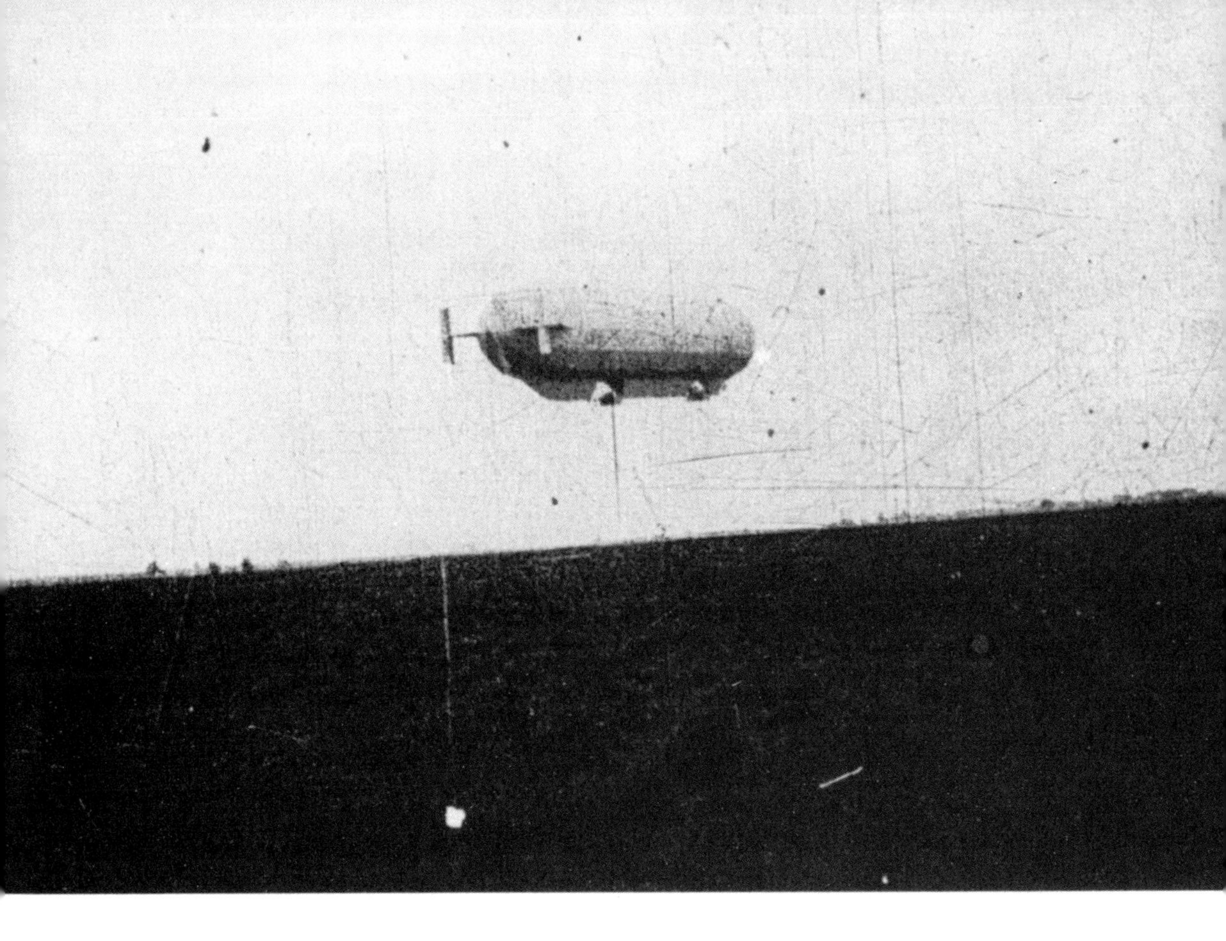

she left them up in the air

Primo Tempo
Sua madre è morta che lei aveva due anni.
Poco dopo, lo stesso anno, l'America entró in guerra.
A nove anni le morí il padre.
Erano molto noti in società e molto simpatici. Lei non ricorda niente.
Lei continuava a giocare agli indiani e cowboys.
Passarono parate
e molte notti.
Suo padre guidava un camion.
Facevano passeggiate,
andavano in giro
mentre
altri
morivano.

Senza titolo
Da un diario ha saputo che a sua madre piacevano i films.
Gialli romantici con vecchi attori in bianco e nero.
Il dramma politico negli anni '30 era elegante.
Le migliori erano le storie d'amore.
Ma le madri erano raramente felici
(senza titolo)

Perdeva tutto e dimenticava tutto
Non le piacevano mai le sue case, perdeva tutto e dimenticava tutto.
Loro erano tutti vecchi ricchi del Sud e lei era proprio matta.
Sua madre citava la Bibbia e ospiti venivano dall'Europa per fare
delle sedute.
Il suo quinto marito era un carpentiere che preferiva stare nudo sulle
scale del terzo piano.
I figli erano eleganti e si erano sposati tardi.
Grumi di sangue erano saliti al polmone. Altri le avevano eliminato
le due gambe.

Lui era romantico
Lui era romantico con molte donne,
beveva molto,
si batteva accanto agli operai,
ai soldati,
e guardava, più tardi, passare i generali.
L'America aveva vinto la guerra.

Per aria
Incontró un meccanico greco mentre stava cercando una Porsche.
Prima e dopo, uno scienziato astro-fisico viveva in una casa con
ascensore nei pressi del Campus.
Uno spagnolo economista rivoluzionario la presentó al figlio unico
d'un Lord inglese eroe dell'aviazione morto.
A N.Y. un pubblicista-poeta in declino la presentó a uomini rimar-
chevoli.
Ma, dopo la rivoluzione
li lasció tutti per aria.

STEPHANIE OURSLER nata a Baltimora, Maryland (U.S.A.) nel 1938, ha studiato al Goucher College, al Pratt Institut d'Arte. Si è laureata all'Università George Washington, ha insegnato Letteratura Americana alla stessa Università.
Ha pubblicato suoi racconti sulle riviste di letteratura: « Antioch Review » e « Evergreen Review ».
Nel decennio 1960/70 ha svolto attività quale organizzatrice incaricata nei movimenti politici americani « Lotta per i Diritti Civili » « Sindacato per l'Assistenza Lavoratori » e « Partito per la Pace e la Libertà », « Movimento per la Liberazione della Donna ».

Ha esposto in mostre personali:

1972 - Galleria « Il Giorno » - Milano.
1973 - Galleria dei Duchi - Spoleto (Festival dei due Mondi).
1974 - Galleria Matuzia - Sanremo.

In mostre collettive:

1971 - Premio Città di Termoli
1972 - Galleria « Il Salotto » - Como
1972 - Galleria Barozzi - Venezia
1972 - Premio Città di Termoli
1973 - Premio Città di Termoli
1974 - Capitolium - Palazzo Braschi - Roma
1974 - American Pie - Roma
1974 - Xe Biennale International d'Art - Menton
1974 - Mostra d'Arte Sacra - Ferrara

Sue opere sono state premiate al « Premio città di Termoli » nel 1971 e nel 1973.
Vive e lavora a Roma e a New York.

« IL PASQUINO »
GALLERIA INTERNAZIONALE D'ARTE MODERNA
Via del Governo Vecchio, 73 - ROMA
26 marzo 1975

T.D.B. - Via Prenestina 468 - 00171 Roma

The Rag Picker
By Giovanna Zapperi

In 1976 Stephanie Oursler clarified her position
of radical de-identification with any established
art group and movement in a letter written
to a German curator working at Berlin's
neue Gesellschaft für bildende Kunst. While
Oursler's work had been discussed in relation
to both narration and feminism, and defined
as conceptual or body art, the artist wanted her
activity to be understood outside of established
and restrictive classifications, focusing instead
on the experimental nature of her practice.
She underlined how, "I simply collect things",
including "objects that are normally thrown
away and put them together with thoughts that
are normally thrown away." Oursler felt that
it would only be when "thrashing, [in a space]
where there is an art movement of rag-pickers
[that] I'll finally be at home."[1] Oursler locates
her practice within the space of surplus or
the inessential. Hers are images and thoughts
that she reassembles, bringing them together with
words that describe personal memories. Such
defiance against established artistic categories
was common among the generation of late-1960s,
artists whose practice can be loosely associated
with what Lucy Lippard and others have
described as the conceptual turn.[2] This moment
was marked by a fundamental rupture with
the continuum of modernist paradigms, during
which artists used self-reflexive positioning to
critically examine the conditions through which
artworks were produced and exhibited.

The significance of Oursler's works related to
the second-wave feminist movement has recently
been reassessed, while *5 Cuts* (1975) with its less
obvious reference to politics remains untouched.
The first in her series of three artist books,
5 Cuts was followed by *Un album di violenza*

(An Album of Violence, 1976), a book based on a collection of photographic portraits depicting women subjected to domestic violence, which Oursler had mostly found in the press, and *Il segreto del padiglione d'oro* (The Secret of the Golden Pavilion, 1977), which was an exhibition catalogue-cum-artist book. Despite their differences in addressing political issues, these projects both used found materials to uncover overlooked histories at the intersection of the subjective and collective. Initially conceived as an exhibition, *5 Cuts* comprises a series of black-and-white frames accompanied by handwritten text and organized into five chapters or "cuts". As such, the book's composition was associated with film editing. Indeed, the found images appear as frames that are seemingly related to films and which convey the atmosphere of silent cinema, with its typically expressive gestures and postures. They often appear cropped or scratched. Sometimes the scene is hardly visible, as if the figures have emerged through a fog as shadows or ghosts haunting the viewer. The short texts accompanying the images hint at a non-linear account of a woman's life. It is the text rather than the image that indicates the narrative story of a woman; her biography appears scattered, as if someone were retelling a story heard long ago.

In her preparatory notes for an unpublished interview, Oursler explains that she was primarily interested in arranging "visual images and language, and then mix[ing] them up with a third ingredient (my life) in a way that produces something that was not there before."[3] The use of language, image, and autobiography in her work therefore opens up an imaginary space, one that does not exactly correspond with fiction, but which is able to speak about something broader than personal experience. Oursler was an active participant in the networks

of women's groups in Rome, a city in which she
spent much of her life. Alongside her experiences
of Italy's "long 1968", this was crucial in
the formulation of an artistic vocabulary in
which political issues were addressed amid
a combination of memory, history, and fiction.
More specifically, the experience of *autocoscienza*
(self-awareness) was crucial to her work,
a collective practice that defined the women's
movement in Italy, emphasizing self-narration
and mutual listening.

Born in Baltimore in 1938, Oursler arrived
in Rome in the early 1970s, having left New
York, where she had been an activist in the civil
rights and in the women's liberation movements.
Little else is known about her life and activities
before moving to Italy other than her graduation
from New York's Pratt Art Institute, which
would suggest that she already had an artistic
practice. Oursler traveled to Rome after meeting
the Italian filmmaker Vana Caruso, with whom
she had a relationship. Oursler's friendship
with Caruso and her husband, the artist Giulio
Turcato, played a crucial role in her life over
the following decades. In Rome, Oursler became
involved in the Italian feminist movement,
to which she also contributed as an artist. She
co-founded the Cooperativa del Beato Angelico
in Rome, a women's exhibition space that
opened in 1976 in the street that it was named
after. In keeping with Italian feminism's critique
of equality—its focus was on the importance
of sexual difference—the cooperative tried
to establish an art space that involved artists
and critics, placing women's relations center stage.
Their program linked historical women artists
such as the Italian Baroque painter Artemisia
Gentileschi, with artists in the cooperative,
emphasizing the significance of female genealogies
for contemporary art made by women. Oursler
was also involved with other feminist networks,

most notably the one related to the art dealer, curator, and art critic Romana Loda, who was a champion of women artists in 1970s Italy. They subsequently developed several projects together.

Although primarily conceived as an artistic space, the cooperative also served as a platform for new ideas about the role of women in the arts, some of which were strongly influenced by *autocoscienza*. Other members included the artists Carla Accardi and Suzanne Santoro, both of whom were members of the cooperative, and who were previously part of Rivolta Femminile (Women's Revolt), the first female-only feminist group created in Rome in 1970. The art critic and feminist thinker Carla Lonzi was also involved, whose ideas about women's creativity and autonomy were disseminated via the cooperative.

The practice of *autocoscienza* originated the United States, developing across black liberation groups and women's collectives to focus on inclusion, equal opportunities, and affirmative actions. It took on its own form in Italy, where women moved in a society that structurally rendered them invisible. According to Lonzi, *autocoscienza* was the key to acquiring an autonomous sense of self, an idea that resonated with the cooperative's attempt to establish an art space predicated on women's autonomy and freed from the patriarchal canon of art history.[4] To paraphrase the Italian philosopher and feminist thinker Adriana Cavarero, women were able to create a relational space in which it was possible to give an account of themselves and to promote a political practice based on self-narration.[5] It is as such that *autocoscienza* reverberates within Stephanie Oursler's work of the 1970s, particularly in *5 Cuts*, where autobiographical fragments emerge from a dispersed narrative like a series of flashbacks,

expressing what is otherwise left unspoken
and unheard, like "thoughts that are normally
thrown away."

The book opens with a double-page spread
that introduces the main character using text
and image to depict a childhood marked
by the mother's death. In the first image
we see a woman on stage performing before
an orchestra. We wonder whether this is the
mother who "died when she was 2", as the
caption suggests. Throughout the following pages
we learn more about the context in which the
child grew up: "america entered the war later
that same year"; "Her father died when she
was 9"; "Later she continued to play cowboys
and Indians"; "Parades passed", and so on.
The handwritten texts hint at an epoch defined
by war, class struggle, and revolution, situating
the personal story within a wider social and
national framework. Nonetheless, the images
are in no way illustrations of the text. Rather,
they convey the space of the imagination,
sometimes via contradictory juxtapositions.
Take, for example, the image of a group of
men wearing tuxedos, who are gathered around
a table that bears two symbols of a skull and
crossbones. Describing the deceased parents, the
caption beneath reads, "They were very sociable
and loved, she doesn't remember." At the end
of the first cut, another image of the singer
that we encountered at the start (the mother?)
is associated with the evocation of death.
The captions over subsequent pages read:

they took walks   and rides,

            while   others

    died.

Life and death, a love relationship in wartime:
these narrative fragments are presented as
a filmic sequence of fragments, through which
the drama of a life unfolds. Death is very
much present throughout the narrative, not
only because the text so often makes reference
to it, but also because of the loss that is inherent
to the medium of photography, with its ability
to capture what was once there but is now gone.

In Oursler's poetic reckoning with cinema
and autobiography, subjective memories and
temporalities are entwined. The book's division
into five parts or "cuts" seemingly follows
the character's biographical path, which as the
art critic Italo Mussa suggests in his 1975 preface,
progresses from childhood into adulthood. Later
in the book, we discover that "from a diary,
she learned her mother liked the movies", above
which sits the image of a woman alone at night.
Together these convey silent cinema's fascination
with female characters that transgress boundaries
of propriety, most notably via the figure
of the femme fatale. Moreover, the emphasis
on the mother-daughter relation, which recurs
throughout the book, points not only to different
types of drama—the ones that unfold within the
family structure—but also the various female
archetypes that define women by reducing them
to playing specific binary roles.

Not only does *5 Cuts* pay homage to cinema,
it too alludes to the intimacy of a private photo
album. In doing so, it calls attention to how
cinema's visual language structurally connects
imagination and subjectivity. According to
film scholar Annette Kuhn, family photo
albums are sites in which the personal and the
collective come together as memory texts. They
"constantly call to mind the collective nature
of the activity of remembering."[6] Indeed, *5 Cuts'*
compositional narrative connects collective

history and lived experience in a way that
ruptures the traditional division between past,
present, and future. In reassembling found
images with thrown-away words, the book
tells a story that is imaginary in its content
while evoking real emotions and memories
in the viewer. It weaves together the personal
and the political in its combination of textual
and visual languages, all the while channeling
the "monumental revolution" championed
by the Italian feminist collectives of the 1970s,
which, as Stephanie Oursler would put it, strived
to overthrow the ways in which we talk and
write about ourselves as women.

1. Letter addressed to Sarah Schuman from Berlin's nGbK,
October 24, 1976, held in the Stephanie Oursler Archives, Rome.

2. See Lucy Lippard, *Six Years: The Dematerialization of the Art
Object from 1966 to 1972* (London: Studio Vista, 1973).

3. The notes were probably assembled by Stephanie Oursler
in order to answer Simona Weller's inquiry into the life and work
of Italy's women artists. The notes are held in the Stephanie Oursler
Archives, Rome.
See also: Simona Weller, *Il complesso di Michelangelo*
(Chieti: La Nuova Foglio Editrice, 1977).

4. Carla Lonzi, "Mito della proposta culturale", in Carla
Lonzi, Marta Lonzi, and Anna Jaquinta, *La presenza dell'uomo
nel femminismo* (Milan: Rivolta Femminile, 1978), p. 151.

5. Adriana Cavarero, *Tu che mi guardi, tu che mi racconti. Filosofia
della narrazione* (Milan: Feltrinelli, 1997), p. 80.

6. Annette Kuhn, *Family Secrets: Acts of Memory and Imagination*
(London: Verso, 2002 [1995]), p. 6.